BUSINESS PROFESSIONALISM

A BLUEPRINT TO HELP YOU ANALYZE, EQUIP, PLAN, AND SUCCEED IN THE WORKPLACE

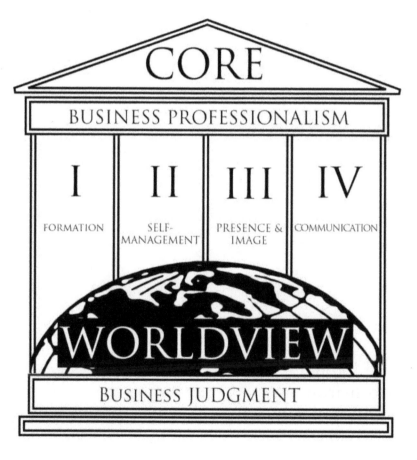

CORE

BUSINESS PROFESSIONALISM

| I | II | III | IV |
| FORMATION | SELF-MANAGEMENT | PRESENCE & IMAGE | COMMUNICATION |

WORLDVIEW

BUSINESS JUDGMENT

BRUCE TODD STROM

with Liza Long

Table of Contents

Table of Contents

DEDICATION

This book is dedicated to my wife Laurie.

ACKNOWLEDGMENTS

I am grateful to my father R. Bruce Strom and friend Ryan Boyer who contributed ideas and provided feedback. Special thanks to Liza Long, a valued colleague who helped me to write and edit the book.

Foreword

Warning–reading this book could change your life.

Are you struggling to achieve your career goals? Do you wish you could be more efficient and productive in the workplace? Have you ever wondered why some people always seem to get ahead in life, and why you aren't one of them?

The secret is business professionalism.

Business professionalism is not a pop psychology "feel-good" message. Nor is it a quick and easy "three steps to wild success" scheme. You've probably already tried those Band-Aid approaches and found that they simply don't work.

Business professionalism is not a goal to be achieved quickly, then forgotten. Professionalism is a lifelong process, founded on four core principles of professional formation, self-management, presence/image, and communication. As you journey through each of these steps, moving from apprentice to master, you will find a practical, ethical, and mindful way to achieve any career goal.

This book is a blueprint for success. It defines the critical need for business professionalism, outlining the ideals behind the theory. These ideals have their roots in antiquity, in the teachings of wise men like Confucius, Plato, and Aquinas. But the book also provides pragmatic solutions to modern problems, and opportunities to develop reflective practices that will result in personal transformation and growth. It even contains some good old-fashioned, common-sense advice.

This book is designed to be read quickly and applied immediately. It can be read in a few hours or over the course of a few days. It contains both academic and common-sense material. But the practice of business professionalism cannot be perfected in a few days, or even in a few years; it requires a lifetime commitment.

If you decide to make that commitment, to apply the four core principles and develop master capabilities in each area, this book could change your life. And if these principles work for you, I hope that you will share. If everyone improved even a little in their practice of business professionalism, I believe that productivity would rise and that employees would be happier, healthier, and more committed to their organization's vision.

I hope this book will cause personal reflection, spark conversations, and maybe even help develop some better business practitioners who will understand the power of positive relationships in the workplace and beyond.

Go ahead…read it at your own risk—the risk of *transformation.*

Bruce Todd Strom, April 2012

About This Book

The weekly sales meeting started five minutes ago. Jennifer rushes in late, her arms full of loose papers. She sinks into a chair near the back of the room, sighs, and pulls out her smartphone, tapping the screen impatiently. Susan, who is leading the meeting, is used to this kind of behavior from Jennifer, and she decides she's not going to let it go un-noticed. Susan glares at the late arrival and says in a voice dripping with sarcasm, "It's good of you to finally join us." Jennifer turns bright red and mumbles something about the weather. The other salespeople are afraid to meet Susan's gaze—they too have been the target of their supervisor's ire. They shuffle their papers in the room's thick silence. As the meeting continues, it's hard for anyone to feel motivated about their work.

What Is Business Professionalism?

We've all probably heard the term *professionalism* at some point in our lives. But what exactly does it mean? When I described the topic of this book to colleagues, I would often get some re-sponse like "my boss/co-workers/colleagues sure could use that book." And in my multiple careers, which have included the mili-tary, private consulting, business, and higher education, I wish I could have shared some of these principles with colleagues and students. This book is intended to provoke thinking and action at the personal level as well as to start conversations with others in groups. It has many uses for both individuals and groups.

I wrote this book to address the kinds of unprofessional situations we all encounter, like the one between Susan and Jennifer above. Lack of professionalism negatively impacts productivity, morale, and self-worth. Organizations that fail to recognize and reward business professionalism are often harmed by disgruntled employees, laissez faire managers, and a general lack of vision. Business professionalism starts at the individual level, but its positive effects spread throughout organizations.

How do you recognize a professional? Often we focus on the external signifiers to determine a person's profession: for example, if we see someone wearing a white lab coat with a stethoscope around her neck, we are likely to conclude that person is a doctor. But in fact, that person could be a medical assistant, a nurse, or a lab assistant. Still, the dress and tools of medical professionals are external signs of their profession.

We use shortcuts like these all the time to make instant decisions about people with whom we interact. Think about the last costume party you attended. Did you recognize roles based on costumes? If you are interviewing for a job, do you usually wear a navy blue suit? Uniform and tools are two ways we can identify a professional.

We also have predetermined ideas about how professionals should act and what they should know. If I asked you to describe a football coach, for example, you might tell me he is athletic, loud, and aggressive. On the other hand, if I asked you to describe a physicist, you might say she wears glasses and uses big words (actually, you would probably identify a physicist as a man, but those attitudes are slowly changing). We expect football coaches to know about game strategies like the famous hook and ladder play that cinched the Boise State Fiesta Bowl victory over Oklahoma in 2007. And we expect physicists to be able to tell us about Higgs-Boson particles and to explain what happens in the Large Hadron Collider.

What is expertise? Who assigns it? How is it assigned? Today, these functions are often ascribed to institutions of higher learning, who are responsible for sharing and assessing knowledge. The quality of an individual's education is often tied to the perceived quality of the institution, which explains why degrees from Ivy League schools land their graduates more interviews. But most people will tell you that after the first job, it's your experience, not your education, that matters most.

The same questions could be asked of business profession-alism. It's easy to call out other people for lack of expertise or professionalism. Judging the appearances and behaviors of business people has become second nature for most of us. How many times have you heard or said, "I wish that person were more professional"? (Or more importantly, how many times has this phrase been uttered about you?)

I wrote this book because I want to create a standard by which business professionalism can be measured. I want to create a framework for self-reflection and growth that can help individuals to recognize their own strengths as well as areas for improvement.

Everyone engages in work and personal ventures that result in measurable outcomes. Goal-oriented behavior is a sine qua non of most organizations today. But while we can measure productivity, or effectiveness at tasks, how can professionalism be evaluated for effectiveness and efficiency in the dynamic business climate of the early twenty-first century?

This book examines the processes and actions available to assure your personal development of business professionalism behaviors, habits, and protocols. The transformational process of professional development is good not only for the individual but also for organizations, as it prepares future leaders and managers and promotes the common good.

It can also be fun.

The Need for Professionalism in Organizations

Why is business professionalism important to organizations? A look at business scandals and crises can give us more than a few reasons.The crash exposed a host of companies who were acting without regard for ethics—think Enron, Arthur Andersen, and WorldCom. In the United States, a fledgling movement that expanded to a peripheral revolution began to demand a more socially conscious business ethic. Grass roots activists became restless, and government began regulating business, with laws like Sarbanes-Oxley, which was designed to create greater transparency, accountability, and disclosure of conflicts of interest. This demand for ethical conduct manifested as political, social, and generational angst on both sides of the political spectrum.

But even those regulations weren't enough. From dotcom bomb to housing market bubble and now to the impending implosion of American student loan debt, a focus on short-term profits at any cost is proving to be costly to businesses, individuals, and society as a whole.

The "greed is good" ethic espoused by fictional Wall Street scion Gordon Gekko in Oliver Stone's classic *Wall Street* has found real-life counterparts in modern CEOs from Lehman Brother's Richard Fuld to Enron's Kenneth Lay.

In theory, capitalism should promote productivity and encourage innovation. As set forth in Adam Smith's seminal *Wealth of Nations*, capitalism is the rising tide that lifts all boats. But too many people have forgotten the "enlightened" part of Smith's self-interest that is essential for ethical capitalism.

Behavioral economists have increasingly pointed to misguided incentives in compensation structure and corporate culture as the roots of our current evil.

Traditionally, business schools have taught their students to focus on the profit motive and the building of individual wealth. The thinking is that focusing on profits and maximizing shareholder value will encompass other virtues such as corporate social responsibility. Modern business schools focus almost exclusively on the quarterly and annual profit and loss statement and balance sheet. But as we have seen, this short-term thinking negates social responsibility, destroys organizations, and has contributed to the rising gap between rich and poor that plagues our once democratic and egalitarian society.

Just as every year is an election year and reasonable legislative action is deferred, every business quarter requires maximum profit, so reasonable pro-business and social initiatives must wait. Both types of delay ultimately injure society.

Individual and corporate thrift became laughable and quaint notions; the desire for liquid cash on hand, regardless of long-term consequences, became a kind of lust, a sine qua non that drove every business decision. As companies who decided to operate this way imploded under the weight of their own dizzying accounting schemes, progressive social and economic thinkers were able to gain a beachhead, both philosophically and practically.

Now is the time to renew the call for ethics, for business professionalism.

Resisting the conventional long-term social contract that exists between corporations and their stakeholders ignores the Darwinian principles under which all organizations operate. In the classical business environment, business is supposed to be the mechanism that provides innovation, change, and growth (creative destructionism). In a classical capitalist model, competition creates better products and services, with the stronger and better overtaking the weaker. Organizations compete for the most talented employees by creating the most attractive work environments and most successful products or services. Growth within this model must be sustainable and strategic if the organization is to survive.

Instead, we find ourselves in an environment where companies exploit loopholes, game markets with inside information, or build their empires on financial houses of cards. Consider Bernie Madoff, who used his position as SEC chair to influence investors who contributed to a Ponzi scheme.

No wonder the Occupy Wall Street movement has gained so much traction in recent years with its platform of "We are the 99 percent."

In case you are wondering, it hasn't always been this way.

And yes, there is a cure. The answer lies in professional ethics, or business professionalism.

We are in the midst of social, economic, technological, and political upheaval. The questionable, old paradigm of immediate profit over long-term business-social responsibility has reached a tipping point. Rampant materialism and consumerism, with their focus on the individual, have eroded our trust in public and private institutions.

People everywhere are unhappy. Organizations everywhere are developing silo mentalities. The ship of capitalism that promised to take us all to a land of plenty is taking on water at an alarming rate.

Smith's invisible hand is replaced with Nash's game theory, which describes decision making strategies in terms of conflict and cooperation of individuals and organizations. The aggregate result of individuals' thinking within the group structure exceeds the aggregate result of individualistic thinking. Since corporations, guilds, unions, and governance all represent different groups, maximizing economic profit for each group requires cooperation and business professionalism, not individualistic "winner-take-all" greed.

How can we accomplish effective change? We must tap into the current energy of change instead of resisting it. By promoting business professionalism at the individual and group level, by incentivizing people to do the right thing, we can regain the promise of capitalism and restore the image of a rising tide that lifts all boats, rather than a sinking ship with too few lifeboats.

How Can This Book Make a Difference?

We have all looked at the appearances and behaviors of business people and thought, "I wish that person were more professional." Consider again the example of Susan and Jennifer given at the beginning of this section. Chances are good that you have sat in a meeting and observed the kind of encounter. Maybe you have even played the role of Jennifer, the unprepared and tardy employee who can't be bothered to pay attention and who does not know how to demonstrate basic respect for her co-workers. Or maybe you were Susan, the unsympathetic manager, who uses sarcasm and fear of punishment to keep your subordinates in line.

On a small scale, both Susan and Jennifer did not behave as business professionals. Their attitudes, if unchecked, create the kind of toxic corporate culture that encourages gossip, harms productivity, and allows employees to justify cutting ethical and professional corners, from taking home office supplies to falsifying report data to lying to regulators.

How do you keep your organization from becoming another Enron or Lehman Brothers? It starts with Susan and Jennifer. It starts with frontline managers, workers, and chief executive officers. It starts with *you*.

Whether or not you work in a profession with clearly defined standards and areas of expertise (such as law and medicine), the term *business professionalism* still applies to you. This book will provide you with a business professional framework for self-reflection and growth. The goal is to give you tools to evaluate yourself and to plan your growth. Be honest with yourself and commit to making changes, even if they aren't easy. Also admit that you can and will make mistakes. But as you move forward from apprenticeship to mastery, you will see positive results.

This book provides a systematic framework for a personal development process that gives for-profit and not-for-profit business professionals at any level a toolbox for success in the dynamic business climate of the twenty-first century. That process includes assessment and continual life growth and improvement. It focuses both on what is (reality) and what could be (theory/ideals).

It is intended to provide you with resources that can formally and informally be used in business professional development. While there is a definite American cultural and economic worldview in the book, the concepts and ideas have global applications.

Why Should You Read This Book?

The primary audience for this book is business professionals, whether they work in corporations or non-profit organizations or are self-employed, including those engaged in business education, training, and development. These professionals include:

- Business practitioners in business and non-profit ventures
- Organizational trainers and learners
- People involved in higher education (teachers and students)
- Business coaches, mentors, and protégés

The target audience for this book is vast and includes tens of thousands of business educators/trainers and millions of their students. It also includes tens of millions of business professionals and hundreds of thousands of business coaches and mentors.

In a sense, everyone from the counter worker at a fast food restaurant to the chief executive of a Fortune 500 company is a business professional. But many of us are not as effective as we need or want to be. Do you want to improve your work and personal relationships? Create new opportunities for promotion and growth? Increase your overall satisfaction with your work? Business professionalism is the secret to your success.

CHAPTER 1

Introduction

Nick was sitting with several co-workers at lunch when the topic of promotions came up in discussion. "I have been with the company the longest in our group and deserve to be promoted to project manager," said Nick. Vicky, Nick's friend, smiled, as she had been making small talk with the retiring project manager earlier that day. The project manager had confided to Vicky that Nick was unprofessional in the way he worked with his peers. Vicky agreed. Nick had always felt that he needed to be aggressive and goal-oriented in his performance to stand out from the crowd. This aggressive behavior was perceived as unprofessional by both Nick's project manager and his peers. What was the evaluation criteria difference between the project manager, Vicky, and Nick? Why the difference in opinion? And what precisely did the project manager mean when he used the term unprofessional?

We all have looked at the appearances and behaviors of business people and thought, "I wish that person were more professional." But what do we really mean? Is business professionalism

1

defined by behavior? Is it appearance? Is it bearing? What about the appropriateness of behavior to situations? How do we define standards for business professionalism? Are our standards too low or too high? Can we trust ourselves to "know it when we see it?"

This section of the book will explore some of those questions and the perceptions that shape our definitions of professionalism.

What Is a Profession?

Professions are recognized disciplines such as education, medicine, law, psychology, and accounting. Any group that self-regulates (requiring members to adhere to standards of conduct reflecting the trust their unique, specialized knowledge requires for meeting some societal need) could be defined as a profession. While the establishment of profession often includes a certification/license process, society imposes only minor limitations in terms of practice and entrusts self-regulation from within the profession to ensure that self-defined standards of professionalism are observed.

What Is Business Professionalism?

Business professionalism is a mindset or judgment system based on self-developed and self - managed knowledge, skills, attitudes, and behaviors. Business professionalism is influenced by work ethic, talent/ability, experience, and the environment. Thus, business professionalism differs from mere compliance with a profession's code of conduct and credentialing: it is a higher standard of ethical behavior to which each individual commits.

The terms *self-developed* and *managed knowledge* above indicate that the definition of business professionalism changes with each profession and each individual. Although both are engaged in selling their expertise, a plumber experiences and portrays business professionalism differently than an attorney. That difference does not imply that an attorney is more "professional" than a plumber or vice versa. Both can exhibit equal levels of business professionalism within their respective fields. Rather, professionalism is a nonjudgmental state of being. We will use the term *professionalism* as a measuring stick in terms of creating your own working definition based on profession, worldview, and experience.

Self-Knowledge Exercise

Read the following questions carefully. Then write down your answers. The act of writing commits the answer in your mind.

- What is your profession?
- What are the knowledge requirements?
- What are the necessary skills?
- What are the ethical requirements?
- What are the acceptable attitudes and behaviors?
- How are these requirements influenced by your talent and experience?
- How does environment (business, social, physical, professional) affect these relationships?
- What professional organization(s) sets and enforces standards for your profession?
- What value does your profession bring to society?
- What is the implied trust agreement between society and your profession?
- What are some of the ethical challenges your profession faces?
- What trade-offs do members of your profession sometimes make in exchange for short-term gains?

The Development of Professions

When we look at a lawyer in her suit or a doctor in his lab coat, we are really looking at the modern manifestation of tribal behavior. Humans are both individuals and members of communities. In ancient times, people formed communities based on affiliations, such as family, tribe, class, and work. As the world developed socially, economically, technologically, and politically, work communities became more specialized and evolved.

Some people worked for organizations. Others were self-employed with skills that were practiced individually, not necessarily as part of a larger work organization. Those self-employed people developed guilds, unions, and professions to deal with economic, technological, social, and political forms and forces that influenced the practice of their activities.

Professions, guilds, and unions promote legitimacy and credibility in the societies in which they exist. They create and maintain special knowledge and skills, codes of conduct, and standards for practice for members of their communities. They also maintain relative autonomy based on the legitimacy and credibility granted to them by society as a whole.

Is business considered a profession, guild, or union? Not really. While there are individuals who belong to work communities that have become professionalized, like accounting, human resources, and finance, many business professionals do not belong to or fit into a formal umbrella organization of business professionals.

Perhaps this lack of industry-wide required knowledge and codes of behavior has led to the current state of crisis in business. In the very early days of the twenty-first century in the United States, there were calls for increased government regulation of business after such events as the Enron crisis and, later, the subprime mortgage bubble that led to an economic downturn in

2008. In fact, the Enron crisis spurred governmental oversight of some business finance functions, as enforced by the Sarbanes-Oxley Act of 2002.

Similarly, from 2008 to 2010, governments throughout the world intervened heavily in the affairs of the private business sector due to a massive global economic crisis whose repercussions are still being felt—especially in the European Union where bailouts to noncompliant Euro countries, including Greece, are threatening economic stability and prosperity throughout the region.

The United States government directly and overtly intervened in the economic cycle by printing money and bailing out corporations with the Troubled Asset Relief Program (TARP) Act of 2007. The recipients of the more than seven hundred billion dollars in taxpayer-funded bailout money included some of the same players whose questionable practices had contributed to the crisis: Goldman Sachs, AIG, and Wells Fargo, to name a few.

For a time, it appeared that the economy was teetering on the brink of a 1929-style economic crash. It appears, however, as we head into the second decade of the twenty-first century, that a primarily capitalistic market economy will survive despite increased government intervention. Business will continue to drive the economy. Businesspeople will continue to operate with considerable autonomy, no matter which political party is in power.

Since we have determined that capitalism has once again survived, we can now explore how the forms and forces that are shaping the American business climate in the second decade of the twenty-first century will affect business professionalism, and how business professionalism can increase productivity, profits, and morale at organizations while simultaneously encouraging organizations to act in socially responsible ways. This book will attempt to lay out a framework for discussion and development.

Business Professional Theory

A hallmark of professionalism is personal autonomy and self-regulation. Using his or her own judgment and common sense, the professional conducts himself or herself in a fashion that earns public trust and personal respect.

As noted previously, business professionalism is a business-like mindset or judgment system based on self-developed and managed knowledge, skills, attitudes, and behaviors and is influenced by work ethic, talent/ability, experience, and the work environment. I encourage you to develop your personal definition of business professionalism as you complete the exercises in this book.

While business professionalism is definitely a practice, it is grounded in ethics theory and has a long history. This section of the chapter will paint a view of professionalism in terms of idealism and theory, giving you a philosophical overview of the concepts that shape our notions of ethical behavior. The focus is on topics that are academic rather than pragmatic in nature. The first topic for consideration is choices and constraints.

Choices and Constraints

We have established that professionalism requires personal autonomy. In other words, the decision to be professional cannot be dictated by an organization. It starts with an individual's choice. In decision theory, choices and constraints define the professional boundaries of this autonomy. How much freedom does the individual enjoy when making choices within the constraints of the business environment? What are those constraints, and how are they defined?

Examples of constraints you might encounter in your own profession include legal regulations, geographic location, standards of practice, corporate culture, and even tradition. These limitations can be formidable and sometimes unassailable adversaries. It is important for you to know the boundaries and constraints of your profession and to honor them.

Practice reflective self-evaluation periodically to assess the range of choices versus environmental constraints. Then, review the vast area that still exists within the boundaries of these limitations to decide what choices are available to you. This process of identifying constraints and working within them helps to reduce the tyranny of the urgent: the idea that we must act now when we don't have all the information we need to make a good decision.

If you want to avoid frustration in your career, you will place emphasis and energy on the choices over which you have control rather than dwelling on environmental constraints over which you have no control. This healthy process of defining boundaries enables the business professional to focus on positive, long-term, profitable attitudes and behaviors, getting to the important tasks and issues; it avoids costly cynicism and negativity, which is usually the result of urgency to act without knowing or understanding constraints.

As Stanford professor Barry Schwartz observes in his book *The Paradox of Choice: Why More Is Less* (2003), "The desire to have it all and the illusion that we can is one of the principal sources of torture of modern affluent free and autonomous thinkers." Learning to identify your constraints and work within them will increase your effectiveness and your sense of well-being.

Individualism and Purpose

Working within the context of choices and constraints, what are the parameters of individualism and purpose?

Purpose and goals construct meaning and give a sense of control for individuals in the otherwise random chaos of life. Purpose defines a person internally, individually, while goals delineate aspirations, life pathways, and life choices. Purpose tells us who we are; goals tell us where we are going.

Some professionals operate as strict entrepreneurs and free agents, while others work in groups or practices. Some live lives of quiet existence. Others seek out and thrive in relationship- or community-oriented environments. Whether you choose one or the other depends on the biological nature and nurture of the individual in psychological and sociological terms. Each individual's lifestyle depends on personal preferences and choices.

All business professionals, even entrepreneurs or independent contractors, work with other people in a dynamic economic environment ruled by a complex set of interactions. Staying focused and keeping an eye on your prize despite the environmental distractions takes relentless stamina and remarkable clarity.

It also requires periodic reassessment. Ideally, the business professional should gauge progress toward goals and work/life balance and engage in self-examination. Are you living the life you chose, or have you strayed off course? This periodic and regular self-examination grounds the business professional in meaning and purpose and allows him or her to evaluate the effectiveness and germaneness of goals.

A note about the goal-setting process: we are all familiar with New Year's resolutions that are abandoned in days or weeks. For example, if you work out regularly, you know that you should find an alternate place for the first few weeks of January. But by February, the gym is clear again. To be successful, a goal must follow some simple criteria. It should be specific, testable, achievable, and relevant (think STAR). You'll have a chance to practice these goals later in the chapter.

During this self-examination, business professionals review their roles in the changing world. An honest examination critically analyzes how well you are adopting and adapting to environmental change, one of the greatest challenges many of us face. How well do individual roles and purposes fit into the larger, complex tapestry of the organizational context? In other words, you'll have the chance to honestly assess what is working for you, and what is not.

Self and Community

While English is one of the most vocabulary-rich languages in the world, it is remarkably poor at offering terms that describe group think or group experience. Without the adjective "mass" (e.g., mass hysteria, mass transit), it is difficult to think of examples. In fact, language itself is a powerful predictor of the degree to which a culture values individualism. Here are a few examples of foreign words that describe group emotions or events:

> Spanish—conmoción is an emotion held in common by the group.
> German—zeitgeist is the prevailing mood of an era.
> New Guinea—mokita is a widely-known, unspoken truth.

Given the individualistic nature of the American culture, which is based on freedom, individual rights, and the individual pursuit of happiness, it is perhaps understandable that we struggle with the notion of community. Where is the bridge that connects personal values and freedoms with community systems of virtue and justice? We see this question playing out in the political arena as the leaders of both parties move increasingly toward extremism, while the vast majority of Americans continue to inhabit the middle ground that politicians from Eisenhower to Clinton navigated so successfully.

We will now examine some theoretical constructs that help to explain both individual and group behavior. The first theoretical and ideal concept is *rules orientation*. This concept suggests that individual and group behavior is rational, predictable, and certain in terms of fairness and justice.

The second concept is *freewill orientation*. This concept suggests that individuals and groups are free to do or think whatever they want in terms of their behavior. Most business professionals practice *common sense pragmatism,* which applies rules orientation at times and freewill orientation at others. They pick and choose the appropriate ideological construct based on situations.

Two familiar concepts that illustrate common sense pragmatism are Adam Smith's *enlightened self-interest* and Jean Jacques Rousseau's *social contract*. Both Smith and Rousseau were intellectuals during the historical period known as the Enlightenment. Smith famously concerned himself with economic theory, while Rousseau focused on political theory. Enlightened self-interest is primarily freewill oriented. In the theory of the social contract, people conduct business within the choices and constraints of self-interest.

The more rule-oriented theory of the social contract has enabled market capitalism to flourish for centuries. Indeed, as we noted previously, market capitalism works fluidly and efficiently within the construct of social contract theory—it is only when corporate social responsibility is ignored that our market economy faces a crisis.

In theory, this linked model of enlightened self-interest and social contract both promotes and constrains consumer and merchant behavior. When business professionals break the principles of that convention, severe consequences follow, including compromised credibility and trust, as we saw with the US banking industry bailouts of 2007.

You may ask, what drives self-interest? Let's consider three main factors: satisfaction, materialism, and achievement. How much materialism and achievement lead to satisfaction? Does more of either necessarily equal greater satisfaction? At what point does satisfaction plateau or begin to decline? The field of behavioral economics has provided some surprising insights into these questions, noting, for example, that money does in fact buy happiness, but only up to about forty thousand dollars per year. Beyond that amount, people actually suffer a negative correlation with happiness and income. The more money they make, the less happy they are.

The business professional must examine these three factors—satisfaction, materialism, and achievement—and determine his or her own individual levels for successful achievement. What drives and what rewards? Is satisfaction a driver or a reward?

Finally, there are the ideals and theory of power and control in terms of the self and community. How much individual power and control exist in the market economy, and how much power and control do community organizations hold?

In theory and idealism, the United States has a mixed capitalistic market system. Powerful and wealthy individuals and organizations hold significant power and wield control over a disproportionate share of resources in market economies (perhaps leading to the populist Occupy movement's claim that they are "the 99 percent"). Community organizations, both governmental and non-governmental, also have mechanisms of power and control. Examples of community organizations might include churches and synagogues, unions, or law enforcement agencies.

Disconcertingly, there have been episodes in economic and political history where the conditions I just described have caused social chaos as master/slave or ruling class/subject relationships and economic classes developed. Those developments caused market economies to be altered by community forces through legal and social agreements and contracts until the theory and ideal of a middle class emerged.

The economic tensions mentioned were felt in waves internationally in the early part of the twenty-first century in terms of the great economic disaster of 2008. While much of the world remains a relatively mixed market economy in terms of the balance of personal and community power and control, the overall system undeniably received some violent shocks, whose after-effects are still being felt and whose consequences have not yet been determined.

Will the self-interest part of the social contract become more regulated by authorities because some powerful business individuals and groups broke trust with the public by violating the delicate rule and freewill balance that has allowed market economies to exist? At the time this book was written in 2012, international market economies appeared to have survived the meltdown without major transformations. But the future remains uncertain, especially in the European Union where a common currency has proven problematic for member states (Britain's decision not to adopt the Euro seems positively brilliant in light of Greece's financial woes).

In America, the situation is also still developing, and much will depend on the outcome of the 2012 presidential elections where the current president has favored regulating capitalism and his opponent, a veteran of venture capital firms, prefers more unregulated market-based solutions to economic problems.

What is certain, however, is that business professionals need to assess their businesslike mindset or judgment systems in terms of appropriate and enlightened self-interest within the constraints of the social contract. We need to develop our own inviolable code of ethics and conduct and practice what we preach.

Summary

Business professionalism is a mindset or judgment system based on self-developed and self-managed knowledge, skills, attitudes, and behaviors. As you identify your place in the professional world and learn your profession's expectations of conduct, you can work to develop a personal definition of business professionalism that will guide your behavior. A key part of this development process is recognizing what drives you to achieve your goals. Understanding the roles of enlightened self interest and social contract will help you to clarify your values. Another critical part of business professionalism is developing and living a code of ethics and conduct, which we will discuss at length later in this book.

In the following chapters, I will outline four core principles that will help to guide you in your practice of business professionalism.

Further Reading

Covey, Stephen R., *The 7 Habits of Highly Effective People: Restoring the Character Ethic,* New York: Simon & Schuster, 1990.

Dembinski, Paul H., Lager, Carol., Cornford, Andrew, and Bonvin, Jean-Michel (eds.). *Enron and World Finance: A Case Study in Ethics.* New York: Palgrave, 2006.

Gilbert, Daniel. *Stumbling on Happiness,* New York: Knopf, 2006

Huevel, Katrina. *Meltdown: How Greed and Corruption Shattered our Financial System and How We Can Recover.* New York: Nation Books, 2009.

Smith, Adam. *An Inquiry into the Nature and Causes of the Wealth of Nations.* Chicago, IL: University of Chicago Press, 1952.

∾ EXERCISE ONE ∾

Use the STAR (specific, testable, achievable, relevant) model to set a professional goal for yourself. Use the Internet to research other goal-setting models.

∾ EXERCISE TWO ✑

- Using your own profession as a guideline, create a hypothetical code of ethics for an illegal activity, like bookmaking, moon shining, or loan sharking. What is the difference between *ethical* and *legal* constraints? Can a principle be both ethical and legal? For example, "first, do no harm" speaks to an ethical issue and a legal issue. Your intent in action is very important. For more information, preview Chapter 10 which contains an ethics primer.

Give these questions some time to percolate; take a walk and consider the consequences of your answers.

Matrix	Ethical	Not ethical
Legal	Business Professionalism	Dishonorable
Not Legal	Non-compliant	Criminal

Ethical/Legal Matrix

Business professionalism is both legal and ethical. The other three quadrants are self-explanatory.

CHAPTER 2

The Fundamentals

Richard is a new account manager at a small tech company that special-izes in providing SaaS (Software as a Service) solutions to small and mid-sized companies. A local yoga studio wants to establish a stronger web presence and has come to Richard's company for help in creating an internet-based customer management system to track their clients' information and preferences and to establish better communication with their customers. Richard has a strong programming background and loves to architect solutions for clients. He creates a proposal that sug-gests an expensive new website and a custom-created CRM solution that is beyond the scope of the clients' needs. Pam, his supervisor, sug-gests that Richard has forgotten the fundamentals in his approach to the yoga studio. What does she mean?

In Chapter One, we defined business professionalism as a businesslike mindset or judgment system based on self-devel-oped and managed knowledge, skills, attitudes, and behaviors.

Business professionalism is also influenced by work ethic, talent/ability, experience, and the environment. Chapter Two introduces the idea of fundamentals, preparing you to learn the four core principles you will use to develop your own business professionalism.

Strong foundations support structures. Foundations include practices and drills designed to strengthen people physically, mentally, and spiritually. If you ever have the opportunity to observe a professional athletic team practice, do it. Professional athletic coaches spend the majority of time working on their athletes' fundamental skills. Basketball player Julius Erving (aka Dr. J) famously said that "I had to spend countless hours, above and beyond the basic time, to try and perfect the fundamentals."

Why do the pros in any profession—the people who are truly at the top of their game—spend so much time on the basics? Because they know that fundamentals must be ingrained and practiced every day, as constant reminders of basic execution, to create a support for more complicated tasks.

Strong fundamentals and foundations are critically, vitally important to your success. When you ignore the basics, when the fundamentals collapse, decisions too often become urgent problems. Individuals acting with a sense of urgency can destroy companies, careers, and fortunes: consider the example of Swiss bank USB's rogue trader Kweku Adoboli who single-handedly lost two billion dollars in assets. If you make sure to do the important things, the urgent need to act without considering the consequences will be minimized.

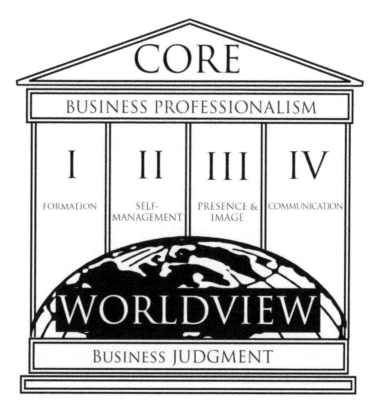

Business Professional Development and Discussion Model

Foundation and Framework

Two major fundamental elements in business involve the mindset and business judgment of the individual or organization. In Richard's case, he approached his client's problem with the mindset of a programmer rather than as a customer relations specialist. When considering your own fundamentals, you should establish a mindset that is appropriate to your role.

Developing a business mindset requires a lifelong commitment. Formal education, the informal process of trial and error, rational thinking, and logic combine as important elements of the business mindset. While you cannot replace intuition and common sense when approaching business issues, you also need evidence-based practices and educational resources. Developing a business mindset is both an art and a science.

Another name for business judgment is *shrewdness*. Shrewd decision makers know value when they see it. That ability to instantly recognize intrinsic value, even in rough diamonds, is a skill that is honed through education and experience. But as noted above, it also depends on intuition. As Malcolm Gladwell points out in *Blink* (2006), our first instincts, combined with a wealth of experience and knowledge, can powerfully shape our ability to make good decisions.

Development of business judgment, or shrewdness, blends nature and nurture. While it appears that some business judgment is biologically based in terms of disposition and emotional/ social acumen, apparently a significant amount of business judgment develops through the process of trial and error and through environmental interactions. Common sense, like business professionalism, possesses subjective components, meaning that the observer often decides whether or not the action taken demonstrated common sense. Paying attention to feedback, both positive and negative, from peers and mentors can help you to build a solid foundation of common sense that will guide your actions.

Worldview

Another fundamental is your worldview, or the generalizations you use to describe and make sense of your environment. Business professionals' worldviews affect their ideals and understanding. Social scientists have observed that we tend to pay attention to information that confirms our worldviews while ignoring disconfirming information, often to our detriment.

Some business professionals hold well-defined and absolute frames of reference. For example, George W. Bush and Steve Jobs, while very different in their goals, both viewed the world in terms of absolutes. Other professionals are intentional in terms of their worldview, striving consciously to create a sense of purpose—think Gandhi or Mother Teresa.

Some professionals serendipitously develop their worldview on the fly, altering their understanding to fit their current situations. This type of professional works well in the technology sector, where rapid changes and advancements lead to frequent paradigm shifts. Still others are relativistic in terms of frames of reference, ideals, and views.

In simple terms, your worldview is your context. It is a powerful force for shaping your attitudes, behaviors, and the conduct in the business environment. Richard viewed his client's problem with a programmer's worldview, providing an elegant but over-the-top solution. If he had used a customer service worldview, he would have realized that the small yoga studio would be best served by inexpensive modifications to existing company customer relations management software that could be implemented almost immediately. Our worldview determines how we approach and solve problems.

For example, consider a statement you probably know to be true: the sun rises in the east and sets in the west. Is this statement really true? Based on our observations, we can say yes, the statement is true. We watch the sun rise in the east, chart its progress across the dome-shaped sky, and enjoy the brilliant hues as it sinks below the western horizon.

But scientifically, factually, the sun neither rises nor sets: it remains fixed in space, and the illusion of movement across the sky is created by the earth's rotation.

To give another example, fundamentally, in business, the dictum "buy low and sell high" is considered to be sound investment advice. Squeezing quality suppliers into bankruptcy by paying too little for their products, however, is counterproductive, as companies like Wal-Mart are learning. On the other hand, selling your product or service for too much literally begs for competition. What is the optimal price point?

The answer is: it depends. Trial and error, market constraints, and illusive psychological factors such as brand influence all play a part in determining price. At the high end of the luxury goods market, for example, where status is critical, a Hermès Birkin handbag retails for $120,000—more than many Americans pay for a house. New York socialite Muffie Potter Aston owns several of them.

So how do you define *your* worldview? The Self-Knowledge Exercise later in this chapter will guide you through the process of creating a worldview with intention. You may want to take a few minutes to look over this exercise now. Set aside a window of uninterrupted time when you can complete the exercise. This act takes courage and may push you beyond your comfort zone. It will cause you to question your world. How does it really work? Don't be afraid if the answers surprise and astound you.

Creating a worldview with intention can be an uncomfortable process because it requires you to challenge your cherished assumptions about the world and your place in it. Consider the 1999 science fiction classic *The Matrix,* where a young man learns that everything he assumed to be true about his life is false, that his "world" is actually a computer construct, and that reality is a harsh dystopian world where human beings, far from being the center of the universe, are merely organic batteries. *The Matrix* is a modern retelling of Plato's "Allegory of the Cave," where Socrates explains the process of constructing a worldview with intention as well as the challenges enlightened people face when dealing with peers who actually prefer to live in a cave of ignorant certainty.

But creating a worldview with intention is an essential part of achieving your potential as a business professional. As you engage in the process, you will learn to separate facts from rumors, assumptions, or prejudices. The philosophical branch known as epistemology examines how we know what we know. Too often, we take convenient shortcuts to "knowledge" rather than working for the truth. Many more mysteries exist than verified, universal facts. Do not assume to know anything—verify.

Creating a worldview with intention will provide you with the foundation you need to become a business professional. As you question your assumptions and test your boundaries, incorporate your observations and conclusions into your true baseline. Use this new reality as your foundation, and measure from that starting point.

Self-Knowledge Exercise

Developing a worldview with intention requires you to engage in the following four steps:

- Question common knowledge, not common sense.
- Cultivate a deep, fundamental understanding of your world.
- Eliminate preconceived notions.
- Define a true foundation from which you measure your progress.

In order to develop your worldview, it's a good idea to see where you are today. Consider your answers to the following questions:

- Do you affiliate with an organized religion? If so, which one? How closely do you align yourself with your religion's teachings and leaders?

- Do you belong to a political party? If so, which one? Do you feel that your leaders represent your views? Do you feel comfortable discussing politics with others who do not share your views?
- List any community organizations in which you are currently active. How do these organizations influence your worldview?
- Describe your level of commitment to your current organization. Do enjoy your work? Your managers? Your co-workers?
- Which of the following statements best represents your views about other people?

  a) I believe that people are essentially good and will try to do the right thing when given the opportunity.
  b) I believe that people act in their own self-interests and will put those self-interests ahead of doing the right thing.

Action Plan

See Appendix J to work on your personal action plan.

Planning and Development

This book advocates intentionally self-developed and managed knowledge, skills, attitudes, and behaviors that are influenced by work ethic, talent and ability, experience, and the environment. Define your foundation, set your goal, and intentionally chart a course through school, training, or professional development. Become a self-advocate for:

- Continuous Process Improvement (review reality periodically and adapt)
- Lifelong Learning

- Purpose-Driven/Goal Orientation
- Reflective Practice
- Standards for Measurement

How can a business professional develop an action plan to develop a business mindset, judgment system, and intentional worldview? This book provides a set of core principles, called the Four Pillars, as a blueprint to build your business professionalism.

Business Professional Core

Every business professional should develop a core set of knowledge, skills, attitudes, and behaviors that guide their practice, including a businesslike mindset. These core competencies should be developed purposefully and with intent.

Acting with appropriate and enlightened self-interest requires an understanding of ethically-driven norms. Developing your core elements is an integral part of forming your professional worldview. Long-term strategic thinking will help you to focus on the important as you learn to shed the shackles of the urgent. This ability to think strategically, with the endgame in mind, will ultimately produce superior outcomes.

The core elements should also contribute to a business professional's purpose or motivation. It will take you time and effort to develop your competency in these areas. But the effort will be worth it: the developed core will guide you, the business professional, on your journey toward goal and career fulfillment. This process inevitably creates healthy professional and personal development.

The core serves as a starting point from which a formal blueprint develops to guide the professional toward meaning and purpose. That blueprint should balance progress with quality assessment. Any business school graduate knows that when growth is too rapid or lacks strategic vision, it runs the risk of destroying an individual or organization. After all, what is cancer but unchecked growth?

As Aesop said of the Tortoise and the Hare, "slow and steady wins the race." Assessment is a key part of the managed growth process. Externalities, such as the progress of key stakeholders, require special monitoring and consideration.

While unchecked or unmanaged growth can result in disaster, you should also beware of stagnation. In nature, there is a well-established life cycle: creation, growth, maturation, and stagnation/death. The core process periodically gauges change, success, or failure of the self within the life cycle, making adjustments as needed to accomplish goals. A true business professional should determine where he or she is in that life cycle process, thus avoiding stagnation.

One good habit involves considering your emotional state and mental attitude regarding your professionalism. Assessing your state of mind against the core elements will help you to determine when you are out of equilibrium. Worry and stress, while short-term motivators, distract us from our true purpose. Don't beat yourself up when you feel stressed; consider it a wake-up call, a reminder to return to the core elements. By addressing and correcting poor behavior as it occurs, you will avoid creating poor habits.

Business Professional Practice

Now that we know some of the theory behind business professionalism, let's explore what we really want to know: How does business professionalism work in the real world? More specifically, how can business professionals transform the ideals and theories mentioned earlier into effective practices?

Let's recall our definition of business professionalism: business professionalism is a businesslike mindset or judgment system based on self-developed and managed knowledge, skills, attitudes, and behaviors and is influenced by work ethic, talent and ability, experience, and the environment.

Theories are interesting. But any business student who has set through a course on macroeconomic theory and then taken an analyst position at a large corporation will tell you that the world of theory does not always correspond to reality. The problem with theory is that it depersonalizes reality. In the realm of theory, it is easy to make decisions about what is right and wrong. But real-world professional practice is a messy swamp of characters with competing motives, unclear incentives, and often inexplicable behavior. How will our ideals and theory of professionalism perform in the real world?

Now we will consider some of the theories and ideals we encountered as they collide with real-world practice.

Choices and Constraints

In the professional theory section of this book, we introduced the concept of choices and constraints, the concept that individuals act as rational decision makers in terms of reflection and choice. We discussed the concepts of autonomy and the promotion of available choices. If you ignore real-world practicalities in favor of theory, you might find yourself dwelling on what ought to be, rather than looking objectively at what is and honestly considering what you can create from that starting point, no matter how poor your initial position looks.

In practical terms, power, control of resources, and politics favor strong, decisive business professionals. Practitioners of the art of shrewd maneuvering or cunning strategy—people who know how to use the system—can and often do succeed over well-meaning, idealistic business professionals armed with behavioral theories. Experienced and talented business professionals with credentials and longevity who are idealistic and theoretical rather than practical and effective can get nudged aside in the eternal competition for power and resources that characterizes most organizations.

You don't want to be the Professor. If you did, you would be busy creating theories of your own. You want to be the Professional.

Here's the hard and perhaps disconcerting reality: business professionals who practice ethical, even idealistic, principles are disadvantaged in the world of work. Again, power, control of resources, and politics favor strong, decisive business professionals. There are also the mitigating circumstances of work ethic, talent and ability, experience, and the environment. Some of these things are within your sphere of control, and some are not.

Accept that you do not control the power brokers, politicians, and manipulators in your organization—those who do not play by your rules, but seem to win anyway. But also accept that they cannot do anything without your empowerment. All it takes to change the culture are a few business professionals who simply do not buy into the notion that less-scrupulous types are superior. As you stand up to people who manipulate in your organization, you will find that power, control of resources, and positive politics become tools of ethical business professionals like you who practice appropriate and enlightened self-interest and adhere to appropriate individual and social norms.

And that reality will be better for everyone.

Individualism and Purpose

In the theory section of this book, we talked about the concept that individuals are motivated by a sense of purpose, by the idea that they have a reason for existence. But who can forget the classic Monty Python illustration of this concept, when, in *Life of Brian,* a crowd shouts in unison, "Yes, we are all individuals." "Well, I'm not," says one loner, who is, ironically, the only one to express a different opinion.

In today's world, everyone is special. Maybe you manage one of those young people who grew up during the time when suddenly self-esteem became the buzzword. Maybe you are one of those young people. Every kid on the soccer team gets a trophy. Every Pinewood Derby car wins a prize.

In reality, it's hard to define a purpose when you're constantly responding to environmental noise. Previous generations struggled to find information; now, the problem is weeding through too much information. How many times have you gone into work with a clear plan for the day, only to find yourself sidetracked and putting off strategic planning, critical assessments, or other vital functions for another day?

The French have a saying, *plus ça change, plus c'est le meme chose,* which can be loosely translated to "the more things change, the more they stay the same." A clear sense of purpose, and the commitment to stick to it no matter what, is the only thing that will enable you to cut through the noise. Purpose translates into productivity and achievement.

Don't let reality destroy your ideals. Even when you have to spend a day putting out fires or tending to menial tasks, keep your purpose firmly fixed in your mind.

Your purpose is why you are here, in your chosen profession. And if you don't know why you are here, you need to either find out why, or find another path.

Self and Community

We looked at the ideas of *rules orientation* and *freewill orientation* with a special consideration for two philosophers: Adam Smith and his *enlightened self interest* and Jean Jacques Rousseau with his *social contract*. In theory, as we discussed, the two should merge seamlessly to create a capitalist society where innovation and productivity are rewarded and a rising tide lifts all boats.

In reality? One word: Enron. Or two words: Goldman Sachs.

Business Professionalism is the Rosetta Stone that can translate the utopian ideals of eighteenth-century philosophers and create a free market utopia populated by people acting in enlightened self-interest with due regard for the social contract.

Summary

The key to becoming an idealistic business professional who succeeds in the real world is intentional professional development by following a blueprint to success based on enlightened self-interest.

Every business professional should develop a core set of knowledge, skills, attitudes, and behaviors that guides his or her practice. These core elements form your professional worldview. The core elements should also contribute to a business professional's purpose or motivation.

Although the process of developing a core is time-consuming and labor-intensive, the core should guide the business professional in creating an effective and satisfying career. The purpose for this process is healthy professional and personal growth and professional development.

The core should be developed into either a formal or informal blueprint to guide the professional toward building a life of meaning and purpose. That blueprint should be a balance between measurement of progress and quality assessment. The business professional must periodically revisit the life cycle to avoid stagnation.

Consider how the following core elements could be built into your blueprint to support a healthy businesslike mindset and judgment system:

- Balancing self-interest (which includes both the profit motive and materialism) with community engagement in terms of healthy, common-sense pragmatism.
- Understanding the environment (social, technical, political, and economic forms and forces).
- Focusing on a healthy work/life balance.
- Developing an effective life change management process.
- Enhancing career knowledge, skills, attitudes, and behavior.
- Improving business effectiveness and efficiency.
- Setting goals and establishing a clear vision.
- Engaging in periodic reflection to learn and grow.
- Becoming a lifelong learner.
- Calibrating the moral compass with real-world practice and common sense.

Now is the time for you to decide what kind of life you want to live. Now is the time to create a worldview with intention. Now is the time to identify the core elements that will enable you to live a happy, productive, satisfying life, both personally and professionally. And it all starts with a simple question that only you can answer: are you living your principles?

Further Reading

Gilbert, Daniel. *Stumbling on Happiness*, New York: Knopf, 2006
Gladwell, Malcolm. Blink: The Power of Thinking without Thinking. New York: Little, Brown and Company, 2005.

Kahneman, Daniel., Diener, Ed., & Schwarz, Norbert (eds). *Well-Being: The Foundations of Hedonic Psychology.* New York: Russell Sage Foundation, 2003.

Rousseau, Jean-Jacques, *'The Social Contract' and Other Later Political Writings*, trans. Victor Gourevitch. Cambridge: Cambridge University Press, 1997.

Schwartz, Barry. *The Paradox of Choice*, New York: Harper Perennial, 2004.

Action Plan
See Appendix K.

✒ EXERCISE ✒

Consider testing your core weekly or monthly:

- Have you been excited to go to work this week? Have you been challenged?
- Did you learn something new and useful during this time period?
- Did you learn new skills? Are you learning new skills? Do you accept the challenge of learning skills and attaining knowledge?
- Have you behaved professionally during this time period?
- Have you thought about or developed a new concept or process, or an improvement to the existing way of doing things?
- Are you doing important things?
- Have you faced anything urgent that had to be done immediately with the risk of severe consequences? How did you handle that "urgent" situation?
- Are you staying in the moment, living now?
- Are you worried? Stressed? If so, what steps are you taking to resolve any issues?

The Four Pillars

In the next few chapters, we will learn the Four Pillars of business professionalism. These pillars support the structure of a healthy businesslike mindset and judgment system. They rest on an intentional worldview that is based on self-developed and managed knowledge, skills, attitudes, and behaviors for business professionals. Before you proceed, make sure that you have completed the exercises that help you to define your worldview.

The Four Pillars are:

Pillar One: Professional Formation, Chapter 3
Pillar Two: Professional Self-Management, Chapter 4
Pillar Three: Professional Presence/Image, Chapter 5
Pillar Four: Professional Communication, Chapter 6

Each of these pillars has a leveling system of apprentice, journeyman, and master practitioner. As you learn and develop your skills and abilities, you will progress from where you are today to become a master of business professionalism.

CHAPTER 3

Pillar One: Professional Formation

Kaitlin is a twenty-three-year-old recent college graduate. She earned straight As in college and prides herself on being the quickest and smartest person in the room. As a new employee, Kaitlin felt disdain for her more experienced co-workers who small-talked, socialized, and did extra work only to impress the boss. Kaitlin felt that her performance and the high quality of her work were all that mattered. Instead of observing and learning from her peers so that she could fit in to her new organization's unfamiliar culture, she felt she had it all figured out. Kaitlin ignored social cues and norms, blazing her own trail in her interactions with peers. Is Kaitlin exhibiting professional behavior?

Now that we've covered the relevant theory and discussed the core elements that form the foundation of business professionalism, we're ready to explore the first pillar of our blueprint:

professional formation. This chapter explains the concept of professional formation and presents a development model you can follow. We will also learn about universal professional development characteristics: knowledge, skills, attitudes, and behaviors.

Professional formation is the process of purpose-driven development and growth. Professional formation may be formal or informal in nature, but the underlying sense of purpose always drives the desire to develop. As you progress through clearly defined stages, you will develop your knowledge, skills, attitudes, and behaviors through exercises designed to measure and assess your progress.

Development Model/Process

Growth and improvement don't happen by accident. Business professionals purposefully plan for development, improvement, and growth. As a committed business professional, you are never "done" with the process of learning and improving—both new practitioners and seasoned veterans can grow and develop in their careers.

Some goals of development include:

- Continuous Process Improvement
- Lifelong Learning
- Purpose-Driven/Goal Orientation
- Reflective Practice
- Mentoring Relationships
- Standards for Measurement

The model/process illustrated graphically below is intended to be applied to all audiences. These might include:

- Formal organizations (e.g., your workplace)

- Business associations or disciplines
- Informal business relationships (e.g., self-employed entre-preneurs and independent contractors)

The process of professional formation can and should be both formal and informal. It can be self-motivated or required by your organization. Education—on-the-job training—for journeymen and masters in organizations, associations, or disciplines is an essential part of the formation process. Equally important are coaching and mentoring relationships: at all stages, these rela-tionships are a powerful tool in effective professional formation.

The model below can be implemented by leaders and manag-ers, initiated informally by individuals in different roles, and/or are initiated by a business professional seeking formal entry into the formation process.

Business Professional Development Model

Roles in the Model/Process

Apprentice

An apprentice is at the first stage of professional formation. Apprentices may be recent college graduates who have just joined an organization, lateral transfers who need to learn a new organizational culture, or people who are retooling their skills for a new career. According to US Bureau of Labor statistics, the average American worker changes jobs seven to eleven times and careers three to five times in his or her professional life. In fact, one 2012 *Fast Company* article on the subject suggested that the average career is now just four years long!

You will return to the apprentice stage of professional formation any time you make a significant change to your professional activities—when you move from an organization to private, independent consulting, for example.

Ideally, apprentices are linked to mentors who promote their learning and development; however, the term is expanded here to include any business professional new to the organization and/ or field on a steep learning curve in terms of culture and skills. The apprentice, by this definition, should seek out more than on-the-job training (OJT), formal training, and/or informal training sessions. Informal activities, such as observing peer interactions, is an important part of this stage.

In the example that opened this chapter, we met Kaitlin, a bright, dedicated new employee. While Kaitlin could certainly benefit from formal training, she should focus her professional formation on more informal peer observation. Learning to respect her peers and understanding her organizational culture are essential to Kaitlin's progress in professional formation.

When you're new to an organization, it can be hard to seek out mentors. But perhaps no activity is more important to your professional formation. New business professionals need to identify and promote relationships with journeymen and masters who can share not only practical knowledge but more informal organizational culture. There's a term for this kind of purpose-driven relationship building, both in and outside organizations. It's called networking, and like any business skill, it takes practice.

If you're at the journeyman or master stage of your professional formation, you might wonder why you need to take on the additional work of mentoring an apprentice. More senior workers benefit from mentoring relationships in several ways. Sharing knowledge is a powerful way for the teacher to learn and improve skills. Subordinates who know the senior's techniques can fill in for you on more minor tasks, freeing you to perform more important and profitable work. When you mentor, you'll experience a positive emotional boost for helping someone.

Finally, by acting as a mentor, you're "paying it forward." If you think about it, you probably did not reach the journeyman or master stage of professional formation without the advice and coaching of a mentor. As you in turn act the role, you are showing gratitude to your own professional mentors and carrying on a tradition that improves your entire organization.

As an apprentice, Kaitlin (and you) should identify potential professional mentors in her organization. Taking their advice and learning to fit in with her organizational culture will enhance her natural skills and abilities, making her a more effective and satisfied employee.

Journeyman

A journeyman is a business professional with experience within the organization and/or in the field: a competent technician, proficient and conversant in his or her field, who is able to communicate well with team members and work patiently through challenges. These skills are required of a good teacher and mentor. In order for the apprentice to develop skills and measure performance, his or her journeyman mentor monitors the work day.

As mid-level, mid-career specialists, journeymen do the heavy lifting in most organizations. Training apprentices alleviates the workload and frees time for strategic planning and promotion-worthy tasks.

Journeymen learn from masters above and teach apprentices below in our model. This combination of both receiving and delivering mentoring develops skills quickly, sets knowledge well, and serves business continuity.

Master

Experienced both within the organization and/or in the field, a master is either an informal or formal leader within his or her organization. Influential and well respected in the organization and/or field, the master is trustworthy, ethical, and emotionally and socially well-adjusted. Masters are truly at the top of their game.

But Masters also understand the need for life-long learning. There are always new skills to acquire, new ideas to consider, new challenges to tackle. A Master is never complacent; he or she always seeks opportunities for self-reflection, improvement, and growth. Achieving this level of competence is correlated with increased happiness and a sense of purpose in the world. Because they have moved beyond their own egos, Masters are sometimes called Transformational Leaders.

The master understands the importance of vision and strategy in crafting goals and the value of patience with long-term projects. He/she embraces opportunities to mentor and coach journeymen and to ensure that apprentices also have mentors.

Benefits of the Three-Tiered Contributor Model

In this three-tiered system—apprentice, journeyman, master— contributors at all levels grow and improve as they participate in the development life cycle. This model benefits both the individual and the organization because:

- There is a sense of shared accomplishment and achievement.

- The model creates more engaged and connected business professionals.
- The model provides a mechanism for successful business continuity.

Human resource professionals within organizations would be well-advised to consider adopting this model. According to Robert Solow, a Nobel Prize winner in economics, human resource development pays the best return on investment for any business. The resources invested by businesses and individuals return on investment in terms of increased productivity and performance (effectiveness).

Assessment/Evaluation

Complete the following three levels of assessment/evaluation based on the model above. It is important that you choose honest people who can give you sincere feedback for this assignment.

Individual
See Appendix G. Reflective practice based on core principles.

Master/Peer
See Appendix H. Requested from a trusted advisor/mentor/peer.

360-Degree Assessment
See Appendix I. Requested from key trusted people around you.

Once you know where you stand, you can chart a course for your development. The following are some development opportunities.

Knowledge

You can never know too much, especially in a global, hyper-connected business environment. Business professionals should practice continuous process improvement with their knowledge management. Maintaining current knowledge and stretching in new areas will set you apart from others in your field and keep you on the cutting edge of advancements and innovations. Many professions require continuing education to maintain a professional status for precisely this reason.

There are two basic ways to improve your knowledge base. The first is *formal* and consists of structured training sessions often described under the rubric of professional education or continuing education. Examples of formal knowledge management include:

- Continuing education to fulfill professional association licensing requirements
- Certifications in relevant disciplines
- Knowledge updates and refresher courses
- Professional designations
- Advanced academic degrees

There are also numerous *informal* learning opportunities, which are less structured and often more accessible. Some of these might include:

- On-the-job training
- Apprenticeship
- Experience
- Safety meetings
- Professional roundtables or brown-bag sessions
- Lecture series
- Conversations with industry experts
- Trade journals

Skills

Skills are practical and measurable manifestations of knowledge. Skills enable business professionals to accomplish goals and objectives. The current trend is to use the term *expertise.* In this rapidly changing world, it pays to become a generalist. Acquire the necessary skills to fill-in for nearly any job description, and you'll make yourself a valuable resource to any organization. Being a jack-of-all-trades also helps you to understand the business system from other employees' perspectives and to see how your organization's parts contribute to make a whole.

There are no "wrong" or "useless" skills. A friend of mine learned to solve the Rubik's Cube because she knew that most people in her peer group saw that puzzle as difficult or impossible to solve, requiring genius or special skills. She would solve the cube while waiting in lines or as she traveled on business.

Solving the cube was an esoteric skill, certainly not one required by her job description. But she found that by twisting the cube a few times, she could start a conversation with almost anyone. She made some valuable connections, including the vice president of Monster.com, who was standing behind her in a taxi line—and insisted on both sharing a cab and paying the full fare after their ten-minute conversation. She lists this skill on her resume and always brings a cube to interviews, since she knows she'll be asked to prove it.

As with knowledge, there are three main ways to develop new skills. These are:

Formal—structured sessions with application.
Informal—less structured, lifelong learning opportunities.
OJT—acquiring new skills by actively doing instead of passively participating on the job.

Attitudes

Because they are internal and highly individualized, attitudes are difficult to control and develop. You've probably heard this famous quote: "Whether you think you can or can't, you're right." That quote sums up the huge impact attitude has on business professionalism.

Business professionals must be aware that attitudes affect behaviors and performance. Consider your own co-workers. Do you prefer to work with people who were consistently positive, even in the face of challenges or deadlines? Do your peers treat you with respect? How would you describe your own attitude toward your work and your peers?

Even a single employee with a toxic workplace attitude can hijack good organizations. Companies recognize the poisonous effects of attitudes and are increasingly screening potential employees through personality tests. As a business professional, you should be familiar with the most common tests, which include the MBTI (Myers-Briggs Type Indicator) and the DISC-III profile.

Do you think you can? Or do you think you can't? Your attitude is best observed by reflective practice and carefully solicited feedback from honest and trustworthy colleagues.

Change

Change is an inevitable part of the life cycle. While change is often painful for both individuals and organizations, internally, change means growth. Darwinian theory explains the necessity of change in stark terms: "adapt or die." In business, the same theory holds true. Change may be painful, but change is good. Change is survival.

External changes are ongoing and are beyond your control. You can adapt to change, or you can get left behind. Business professionals who can learn to embrace both internal and external change are survivors.

After all, change is the only constant, right?

Realism

We've all sat in those "vision thing" business meetings where a consultant or distant senior executive outlines sweeping goals for the company: "We're going to be selling soft drinks to robots on Mars by the year 2023," or some such nonsense. A successful business professional is firmly committed to a *realistic* vision of success.

An effective business professional practices realism in planning, organizing, and controlling tasks and projects. Remember the STAR goals we talked about in the first chapter? Specific goals are realistic goals.

The key to realism is practical thinking. You ask yourself, "Will it work?" On the other hand, the opposite of realism is idealism, which is rigid and perfectionist, focusing on *oughts* and *shoulds*. The realist practices in the swampy, steaming, mud-caked jungle of business, with both its attendant risks and rewards.

Why do business professionals need to be realistic? Because the aim of business is to make a profit and not necessarily to meet idealistic goals. At the same time, as we noted in Chapter Two, idealistic goals should be part of the equation. The effective business professional is able to balance realism with idealism to get the job done while also pursuing that "vision thing."

Problem Solving

In ancient Greece, philosophers often focused on the difference between *lexis* (words) and *praxis* (actions). A hero, according to Aristotle, was both a doer of deeds and a speaker of words.

Likewise, business professionals are both doers and thinkers, with an emphasis on action. Both ancient Greek heroes and modern day business professionals have to solve problems.

Business professionals should actively develop their problem solving skills, adopting analytic tools that, coupled with intuition, will help them to make sound and effective decisions. The shrewd business professional avoids "analysis paralysis" and makes research actionable—he or she knows how to satisfice, to borrow a term from behavioral economics, rather than maximize. A satisficer is able to do enough research to find a practical solution, while a maximizer often gets bogged down in searching for the best, most perfect solution.

While the idea of an all-wise philosopher king sounds good in theory, in the real world, business professionals must be realistic problem solvers more than idealists. Problem solving is a skill, and like any skill, your abilities will improve with practice. As you develop decision making abilities in less important situations, you will find that you are better able to handle more complex ones.

Introversion/Extroversion

A word about these two terms: introversion and extroversion may not mean what you think they mean. Both introverts and extroverts like other people just fine, and both can develop appropriate social skills. But introverts draw their energy from solitude—so-called "cave time"—while extroverts draw their energy from associating with others.

On the surface, since business is about relationships, it would seem that extroverts would have the odds stacked in their favor. This is not necessarily the case. Both introverted and extroverted business professionals may need to make some adjustments to their relationship and communication styles.

Business professionals who tend to be introverted should focus on developing adequate interpersonal and social skills to engage customers and clients effectively. Conversely, extroverted individuals need to learn to set appropriate boundaries in their interactions with customers and clients.

Knowing what "type" of person you are is the first step to improving your skills in this area. Take a personality assessment and study the results. Also, consider your interactions with your co-workers. I once managed two employees who had a difficult time connecting. Both had come to me individually with concerns about working with each other, even though both expressed great respect for each other's knowledge, skills, and abilities.

"He calls and just talks," Melanie said in exasperation. "I feel like he doesn't trust me to understand the scope of the project. And I never know exactly what he wants."

"I feel like I'm always bugging her and she never has time for me," Ken confided. "I feel like she doesn't value my opinion."

As it turns out, Melanie was an introvert. She liked to be given clear, concise directions, then left alone to come up with work product. Ken was a classic extrovert, needing someone to bounce his ideas off of. I called them both into my office and explained my insight. We all laughed in relief. Both Melanie and Ken learned to adapt their communication styles to suit each other's needs.

"Just to be clear, are we just brainstorming here?" Melanie would laugh when Ken started to wax rhapsodic about a project. And Ken learned to give Melanie the concise, clear directions and the space that she needed.

If you are struggling with introversion or extroversion issues, consider finding a good business coach who can work with either type of personality to help you adjust your work behavior appropriately. Role playing, self-assessment, and coaching can all play a part in your success, and all are well worth the investment. Poor people skills will kill otherwise promising business careers.

Judging

"Don't judge a book by its cover." You've probably heard a message about the importance of avoiding judging others several times in your life. And what an important message that is for the business professional!

The effective business professional must never rush to judge people or situations without careful scrutiny of appropriate and relevant evidence. As we said earlier, we all have a tendency to look for evidence that confirms our beliefs and to avoid evidence that disconfirms them. While true objectivity is probably an impossible goal, it's important to be as impartial as possible when faced with a situation that could destroy a career or harm an organization.

Remember that there are always at least as many sides to a story as there are stakeholders. As you consider the evidence, your process should be internal to avoid creating ill will with associates and/or clients and customers. Remember, once an accusation has been made openly, it cannot be taken back. The shrewd business professional attempts to rein in emotion and practice constraint and circumspection in all circumstances. As you grow in this area, you will win the respect of colleagues, clients, and other professionals who will know that they can trust you to be fair.

Perceptions

Our ability to make snap judgments developed as a powerful survival instinct. But in the complex world we now inhabit, we have to force ourselves to remember that appearances can be deceiving in business transactions. Effective business professionals try to avoid rash decisions based on general perceptions and emotions—good feelings. They try to make judgments based on facts and evidence, not emotions or good will.

Consider the well-known case of Bernie Madoff, former chairperson of the NASDAQ stock exchange, who will spend the rest of his life in prison for running a fifty-billion-dollar Ponzi scheme that many consider to be the most egregious case of financial fraud in America's history. Madoff was so successful because he was perceived as trustworthy. Regulators overlooked the "too good to be true" aspects of his asset management business, even when a simple examination of his stock records would have revealed the fraud.

As a business professional, you must remember that perception is not always reality. Remember this Arab proverb: "Trust in God, but tie your camel tight."

Positive, Negative, and Realistic Thinking

Although it is easy to be cynical and negative based on the current economic conditions and the seemingly unchecked plague of other people's unprofessional behavior, the effective business professional should try to avoid negative thinking and remain rational and realistic in their approach to life.

Positive thinking certainly has its place, judging by the book titles in the self-help section. While some business gurus teach the power of positive thinking, it is best to be realistic in attempting to meet business goals and objectives. Realism will keep individuals from the bipolar extremes of totally positive and totally negative thinking, helping them to chart a safe course through the swampy world of business.

Realistic thinking starts with control. Honestly consider what is in your control, both internally and externally, and what is not.

If you can't control something, then learn to adapt to it. Positive thinking, just like worry, is about predicting the future, and you can't predict the future. It's fine to be optimistic, but planning requires thinking through all the possibilities, not wishing on a star that everything will be for the best. An overly positive attitude is nearly always a sign of poor contingency planning.

On the other hand, negativity is toxic and transferable. And it does nothing to solve problems. While overly positive thinking often reflects poor planning, negative thinking is a sign of stagnation. The business professional remains cautiously optimistic, planning for both best- and worst-case scenarios.

Formal or Informal

In the business world, most of the time it is best to conduct oneself in a more formal, businesslike manner. This behavior is less likely to open up the business professional to allegations of inappropriate behavior or involvement in messy emotional entanglements.

(Yes, I am saying don't date people you work with. It rarely ends well for either party.)

Although some business cultures, most notably in the technology sector, have become more casual, business professionals wearing khakis and polo shirts should still conduct themselves in a more formal manner, even within a casual environment, to avoid communication issues and missteps. The more casual relationships become, the more opportunities there are for individual and social misunderstandings that can harm important business relationships.

Remember that you are a representative of your organization and you should remain businesslike in all public forums. While at charity events, concerts, and even out shopping, you do not know who is observing your behavior and dress. It is important to be on your best behavior at all times.

Also, be cautious in your use of social media and technology. While few of us have ever committed a gaffe to rival former US Representative Anthony Weiner's naked picture texts, we could all probably be more careful in the way we use Facebook, Twitter, blogs, and other social media outlets.

Be assured: employers and organizations are watching you. The instant access and quick connectivity of social media make otherwise level-headed people say things they should not say in public forums. Inappropriate Facebook posts have destroyed careers. Don't let a chance comment destroy yours. Remember, Facebook is forever.

Behaviors

One thing that is always within your control is your behavior. Behaviors are often initiated by emotions and feelings. Business professionals should practice balance and monitor their own behaviors, which are best observed by reflective practice and by soliciting feedback from others.

What follows is a brief discussion of common personality types and behaviors that you will encounter in the workplace.

Type A/Type B Personalities

The Type A/Type B theory of personality was originally conceived in the 1950s to test correlation between personality and the risk of coronary heart disease. Though the theory has numerous critics, it has become a kind of cultural shortcut to describe the differences between more rigid and controlling people and more laissez faire, easygoing people.

Type A personalities tend to be excessively control-oriented. They stress order and rules above all else. In contrast, Type B personalities tend to be more relaxed and less stressed about control and order. In fact, the perfect behavior is somewhere in the middle. Aristotle's famous Golden Mean theory, which holds that excellence is attained through moderation, holds true for behavior. Excessively controlling or excessively relaxed behavior is not balanced and can lead to effectiveness and efficiency issues for business professionals.

Rational/Emotional

Passion is important. Honest enthusiasm for what you do will separate you from others in your profession. But the effective business professional knows when to be rational and when to be emotional. There is a time and place for exercising control and demonstrating passion. You should work on developing your situational awareness so you will know which response is most appropriate.

In general, you should control the role of your emotions in business affairs and use the power of emotions to feed drive and passion when needed. An example of emotional power is creativity/innovation. An example of rational thinking is analysis. Both are important.

Decisive/Non-Committal

As a generality, confidence in decision making is an admired trait and one that people associate with effective leadership. But decisive people do not always make good decisions.

A student of mine once told me the following anecdote about decision making:

My senior year in high school, I was selected to go to Girls State, a true honor. I roomed in a dormitory with several other girls. Our first night there, we were awakened by the sound of the fire alarm. Without even thinking, I told the other girls,

"Follow me." I led them to the door, and we walked down the hall and took the elevator to the lobby below.

There were several things wrong with this scenario. For starters, you should never open a door into a hallway in a potential fire situation without checking first for heat or smoke. Secondly, under no circumstances should you ever take an elevator when a fire alarm is sounding. If there had really been a fire, my decisive leadership could have gotten all of us killed. I am still astonished that not a single one of those girls, all of them the brightest in the state, even questioned my faulty leadership. They all just followed.

This student's ability to make a quick decision and convince others to follow her lead could have had devastating consequences for the group. On the other hand, failure to act when necessary can also lead to disaster. Noncommittal leaders, who just let things happen rather than making conscious and necessary decisions, are generally ineffective.

Even when decision making does not come naturally, it can be developed with experience and effort. Decision making is a skill. Like any other skill associated with business professionalism, you will improve in this vital area as you practice making good decisions.

Arrogance/Lack of Confidence

Remember Kaitlin, our twenty-three-year-old wunderkind? While confidence is a good trait, when pushed too far, confidence may be perceived as arrogance. The perception that a business professional is arrogant can become an interpersonal and social issue that undercuts effectiveness. While confidence is reassuring, no one likes an arrogant person.

If you struggle with the problems that plagued Kaitlin, work on your presentation style. Try to avoid arrogance whenever possible. Come up with ten great reasons you have to be arrogant. If you can't do it, stop being arrogant and start listening. You'll be amazed how well active listening will work as an antidote to arrogance.

Excuses, Excuses, Excuses

Imagine a world without excuses. Projects would always be done on time and in budget. Employees would be cheerful and punctual every day. Mistakes, though rare, would be honestly owned and corrected in a timely manner.

If you've spent any time in any kind of organization, you know that an excuse-free workplace is a fantasy. Life happens to all of us. People get sick, projects go over budget, tires go flat. That being said, excessive excuses quickly become both an interpersonal and social issue in organizations.

An excuse is a symptom of poor problem-solving skills. As you practice your problem-solving skills, your excuses for delay, nonperformance, or failure will disappear.

Above all, avoid turning yourself into a victim.

A fellow instructor at a college where I once worked frequently missed class for problems ranging from health issues to family emergencies. The instructor constantly complained that he was underpaid and overworked, yet in reality, the other teachers in the department frequently had to cover for him to ensure that students were taught.

At first people were sympathetic to this instructor. "He seems to be so unlucky," we said. But after two years of weathering this man's constant excuses, overwhelming "bad luck," and extreme negativity about the organization, we began to suspect that he thrived on being a victim—that he was in fact a problem.

We all have legitimate emergencies. But learn to solve your own problems, and if you are a manager, be on guard for the "victims" in your organization. At best, their blame-shifting be-havior will hurt morale and negatively impact productivity. At worst, they may succeed in attacking your organization, through lawsuits or other means.

Don't be a victim. Be a problem solver.

Rebels without Causes

Remember the scene in the movie *Jerry McGuire* where Tom Cruise loses his job for standing up for his principles? While nothing in this book suggests that you should check your moral principles at your organization's door (in fact, I am making the exact opposite point), the fact remains that you can't change an organization if you lose your job.

At some point, effective business professionals need to learn to avoid emotional, rebellious tendencies and excesses. If you feel the need to contradict your manager in a public meeting, write yourself a note and speak to her later in private. Most people, your manager probably included, actually appreciate construc-tive feedback. But very few people appreciate personal attacks in a public forum.

If you want to change your organization, or if you have a cre-ative, innovative strategy, frame it and present it carefully and respectfully. Don't be confrontational; it might make a good dra-matic scene in a popular film, but it's a self-destructive, losing strategy for you and your organization.

Power Seeking/Bullying

Some business professionals view seeking and getting power as their ultimate goal. The power they seek, they argue, will make them highly influential and important. This type of self-serving behavior often leads to arrogance and judgmental attitudes.

Power always comes with the high price of responsibility and accountability to stakeholders, a heavier burden than most people can imagine.

Extreme power projection can lead to bullying behavior in the workplace. Bullying may get you short-term results, but it is always a losing strategy long-term. The idea of control is an illusion, and the idea of powerful control is delusional. Use your power to unite your organization's members around a common goal rather than to demonstrate your own glory.

Consider this example: When a CEO flies coach to a meeting because he sent his private jet to transport an employee's sick child to a specialist, he gains power and the organization bonds as a team. When the same CEO fires that employee for missing work to attend to his family emergency, the CEO may believe he's powerful, but he has actually disempowered himself, losing the respect and consent of his many angered employees.

Use power wisely. Bullying and self-serving behavior will ultimately backfire.

Persuading/Manipulating

The line between persuasion and manipulation is narrow. One of my doctoral students in Organizational Leadership once joked that the degree should be renamed "Advanced Manipulation Techniques." On the one hand, business professionals must cultivate the ability to persuade and convince others of the need for goods and/or services.

But where is the line between a successful sales manager and a con artist? People who abuse persuasive behaviors can wander quickly into ambiguous moral and legal territory. Persuasion is perfectly ethical; flimflamming is criminal.

Business professionals persuade. They never mislead or misrepresent their services or products. Those who do may succeed in the short-term, but the market usually discovers misrepresentations quickly.

Build a better mousetrap, and the world will beat a path to your door. Market that mousetrap as a cure for cancer, and you're likely to encounter some problems down the road.

Summary

In this chapter, we learned about the first pillar of the business professionalism core: professional formation. Create a personalized plan to enhance your knowledge and skills, then identify and attack self-defeating behaviors and attitudes. As you progress from apprentice to journeyman to master in your professional formation, you will have the opportunity to seal your knowledge and abilities by sharing what you have learned with others.

Professional formation—developing knowledge and skills, and understanding attitudes and behaviors—requires effective, professional, self-management. In the next chapter, we will cover this second pillar of business professionalism.

Further Reading

Bennis, W. *On Becoming a Leader* (4th ed.). Philadelphia: Basic Books, 2010.

Daft, Richard L. *The Leadership Experience (4th ed.).* Mason, OH: Thomson/Cengage, 2008.

Goleman, Daniel, *Emotional Intelligence*, New York: Bantam, 1997.

Schein, Edgar H., *The Corporate Culture Survival Guide,* A Warren Bennis Book, Jossey-Bass, Inc., 1999.

Senge, Peter M. *The Fifth Discipline: The Art and Practice of the Learning Organization.* New York: Doubleday, 1990.

Solow, Robert M. *The New Industrial State or Son of Affluence.* Indianapolis: Bobbs-Merrill, 1967.

Case Study

Test your knowledge of the concepts covered in this chapter by applying them to the following case study.

Jim was hired out of college business school to work as an entry-level technical recruiter. As a student, he took an unpaid internship in the field. The knowledge and skills he acquired in that internship proved invaluable.

After orientation, his new boss took him around the office to meet his co-workers.

From his internship, Jim had learned to watch office politics. He was given some advice by co-workers during a welcome aboard lunch.

Nan was a fourteen-year veteran of the firm and had twenty years in the field. She was a sales leader, but she was cynical. "Do your job and keep your head down," she told Jim. She encouraged him to stay alert and competitive because winners get commissions and awards. She also advised him to avoid making friends with co-workers. "They are your competition," she warned him.

Nate was a fairly new recruiter who had three years' experience. He told Jim to stay off the boss's radar. "Do your job, and do not play politics," he said. "Be a company man, and you'll do all right."

Jeff was a former manager at the firm. He had twenty-five years' experience in the field, ten at his current firm. He was hired as a manager but decided to take a cut to recruiter last year to be able to spend more time with his family. Jeff's advice to Jim was to seek out a technical expert for questions about the field and to ask for help. "I am here for you with career advice," he said. "Don't be afraid to ask anything."

Sally was an industry veteran with thirty years in human resources and had spent the last four in recruiting. She was sharp and lucid about change in the industry. She seemed competent and confident when dealing with people. She gave Jim a brief history lesson on the field and firm.

Meg was the office busybody. She thought she knew everything about everyone and speculated about office politics freely to whomever would listen. She offered Jim her view of the office.

Based on the material covered in this chapter, which colleagues are most likely to provide Jim with advice and support that will enhance his professional formation? Which co-workers should he identify as potential mentors, and why?

EXERCISE

Take a few hours to develop a professional formation blueprint for yourself.

Where are you on that blueprint now? Where do you want to be? How can you fill that gap? Be specific about professional development, mentoring, and other activities that will help you to reach your goals.

Action Plan
See Appendix A.

CHAPTER 4

Pillar Two: Professional Self-Management

Debby spent over twenty years as a salesperson. She rose to the position of regional sales manager in her organization. How much of the energy and resolve that made her successful in sales would be appropriate in her role as manager, dealing with a new peer group of motivated alpha salespeople at a higher level?

Once you have planned and implemented strategies to succeed in your professional formation, you will turn your attention to the second pillar of business professionalism: professional self-management. In this chapter, we will look at individual self-control and discipline in professional conduct. What is appropriate behavior? And how can you evaluate your own behavior to ensure that it is appropriate?

Assertiveness Model (Shark/Dolphin/Minnow)

Business does not exist in a vacuum. It is part of a larger web of social, political, and economic subsystems. Those subsystems inevitably affect how business is conducted. In organizations and associations and among self-employed business professionals, there are numerous psychological and sociological forces at play. Each business subsystem is a unique environment with its own formal and informal rules and appropriate behaviors. This section will examine power relationships in business subsystems.

The assertiveness model below imagines interpersonal and social power projections as if they were represented by marine life in competition for scarce resources. The focus is on assertiveness. In the model, there is a limited supply of resources to support all the participants.

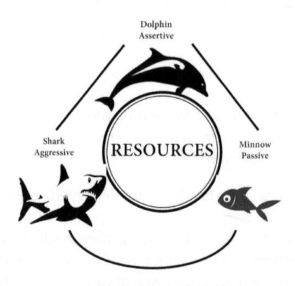

Assertiveness Model (Shark/Dolphin/Minnow)

As we consider each of the groups in the model, think about your own experience in organizations. How do you interact with others when competing for resources?

Minnows

In the model, minnows represent more passive business professionals. These individuals are content to swim in a large school and follow the fish in front of them. They are risk averse and content to play a defined and clearly bounded role in business.

Consider lifetime journeymen or commissioned sales people. These roles support the overall organization, adding to business profit. This business niche requires professionalism and integrity, and some people are comfortable in this role with no aspirations to move beyond the pond. Every business needs and wants minnows.

Dolphins

In the model, dolphins represent assertive and active business professionals. These individuals are adaptable to change and goal oriented. They tend to thrive within small pods of likeminded individuals. Dolphins are capable of taking measured risks and are creative and innovative.

Dolphins feed on available resources, rarely attacking minnows except when necessary. They are adept at protecting themselves and their groups from predatory sharks due to their assertiveness, adaptability, and sense of direction.

Small-business entrepreneurs and enlightened CEOs tend to be dolphins.

Sharks

In the model, sharks represent aggressive and oppressive business professionals. These apex predators exist to feed and grow. They tend to hunt alone but can associate with small groups when it serves their individual interests.

Sharks feed on minnows, may attack dolphins, and consume other available resources when necessary. In fact, sharks have been known to devour all available resources and move on, with devastating implications for organizations.

Observations

The model represents a business organization in terms of a Darwinian food chain. The minnows in the large school of fish represent most business professionals. Unless consumed, they each fill roles and needs in the business environment.

The dolphins represent effective business professionals in terms of power projection and assertiveness. They are adaptable and flexible and use resources wisely. A major asset for dolphins is their ability to assert themselves appropriately in the marketplace. This assertiveness makes them strong like sharks, but they are able to grow and adapt to their environment.

The sharks represent ambitious, power-hungry business professionals. While they appear successful, their aggressive nature consumes most, if not all, of the available resources and is harmful to business itself in the long run.

As you consider your own organization and your role in it, remember that there are individual, psychological, and socio-cultural context factors to consider in any reflective practice model. It's fine to be a minnow, difficult but rewarding to be a dolphin. If you're a shark, you're not in it for the organization. You're in it for yourself.

Now that we have a power relationship model in mind, we will look at some self-management considerations for business professionals.

Appropriate Conduct and Demeanor

At the beginning of this book, we asked, "What is business professionalism?" We discussed the idea that image and behavior determine our notions of business professionals. So what should the effective business professional look and act like?

In practical terms, there are many good books on dressing for success and professional etiquette. But an appropriate response to the question is situational. In general, it is advisable to dress and act up one step from the organization's norm. For example, if everyone at your organization comes to work in blue jeans and T-shirts, you should wear khakis and a collared shirt—one step up from the norm.

Acting and looking like a professional will help you to *be* a professional. In fact, organizations should consider how well their dress codes align with their missions and goals.

A friend of mine attended a court hearing for her name change. Unlike the other participants, she dressed in a conservative business suit for the occasion and was flattered when the judge mistook her for a lawyer and complimented her on taking her court business so seriously.

Other people will judge you by your opinion and demeanor. But more importantly, you will judge yourself. Dress like a business professional, and your chances of acting like a business professional improve astronomically.

Self-Discipline

If you've ever thought about training to run a marathon, you understand the vital importance of self-discipline. Successful marathon runners all have something in common: they have self-discipline, and they know how to pace themselves.

Similarly, the effective business professional is controlled and moderate. He or she is neither too quick nor too slow to speak and act, even when provoked. *Measured* is a good term to remember—and you might even want to practice actual measurement, in the form of a slow deep inhale and even slower exhale before you respond to upsetting or exciting news.

Self-discipline also involves goal setting and accountability as well as good time management skills.

Time Management

Time management and self-discipline are inextricably linked. A good practice of effective business professionals is time orientation. Planning events and creating a schedule when possible and practical can be very helpful.

Managing time effectively is both a science and an art. There are many tools that can help you to manage your time, including increasingly sophisticated calendaring programs.

Your own time-management program should start with honest self-evaluation. Where do you spend your time? How do you handle menial tasks or projects that are necessary but dull? Remember that flexibility is key to effective time management, as are good triage skills: you should practice separating tasks into categories by importance.

If you find that your calendar is full of urgent or time-sensitive projects, you probably are not managing your time well. Consider your habits and make adjustments as necessary.

Resource Management

Remember the shark/dolphin/minnow model that led this chapter? Sharks, minnows, and dolphins are all competing for the same pool of resources but for very different reasons. Your initial access to resources depends on your role in your organization. Your continued access to resources depends on how well you manage them.

When you think of resources, it's natural to equate them with money. After all, your budget and how you allocate it affects your productivity and your ability to accomplish your goals. Wealth is an important resource, both for individuals and organizations. Setting a personal budget and tracking your expenses are good habits to cultivate and will carry over into your professional life.

But there are other kinds of resources: people, for example. Just as you manage your financial budget, you need a system to manage your professional contacts. Social networks have always been important to business professionals. The online component of social networking has vastly improved our ability to manage and connect with people who can help us to meet our goals.

When you think of the term *network hub*, you may visualize a router than sends signals to various places. But increasingly, network hub is being used to describe individuals and organizations who have developed broad and rich social networks. These human network hubs serve the valuable function of connecting people who need each other's skills and expertise.

While the days of the Rolodex are probably past, a tracking system to manage your human resources is vital. LinkedIn is one way that many professionals manage their business connections. E-mail programs also have contact management features. Familiarize yourself with these and spend a few minutes every day reviewing your contacts.

If you don't already do so, get in the habit of carrying business cards and exchanging them at every opportunity. The person seated next to you on an airplane may be the lead to an important supplier. The woman you meet at a social event may be the person who recommends you for your next job. Also, actively network in your community through social and business events. If you don't know where to start, contact your local chamber of commerce.

By managing your financial and human capital, you will be able to meet your professional goals.

Work Ethic

One common feature of all effective business professionals is a good work ethic. While defining this term can be tricky, generally speaking, a work ethic is measured by the effectiveness and efficiency of work product. Work ethic does not necessarily mean spending long hours at the office. It means getting the job done and doing it right. We can measure a person's work ethic in terms of output or productivity. Work ethic can also be measured in terms of work quality.

Successful business professionals find motivations, passion, and drive to get things done. They are also able to manage their work well. Finally, they care about their work, and they want to make a difference. These ingredients combine to create a good work ethic.

Office Politics

Almost three millennia ago, Aristotle, the father of empiricism, noted that "Man is a political animal." People who ignore office politics do so at their own peril. Consider again our shark/dolphin/

minnow model. How well does it apply to your organization? Who are the sharks? The dolphins? The minnows? Where do you fit in?

Effective business professionals know how to navigate the waters of organizational or office politics. Whether they are minnows or dolphins, they understand real power and practical politics, not abstract ideals or theories. Above all, they try to avoid the shark-infested waters of risky and non-productive political entanglements.

Emotional and Social Monitoring

An important part of professional self-management is reflective self-analysis. Have you ever felt like you just can't say the right thing during a social business gathering? Do you struggle with emotional encounters in the workplace? Business professionals should practice reflective analysis during or after emotional or social events.

If you find yourself responding emotionally in a business situation that requires clear-headed thinking and rational judgment, don't be afraid to take a time-out. Breathing slowly through your nose and exhaling with your diaphragm will trigger a parasympathetic nervous system response that will automatically calm you down.

Once you are calm, ask yourself, What triggered those particular emotions or behaviors? If you know that you struggle with social situations, don't avoid them—practice! As you practice professional self-management, you will find that you are better able to control your emotions and behaviors, even in difficult social settings.

Decision Making

Since good decision making is so vital to a business professional's success, we will end our professional self-management chapter with an in-depth exploration of decision making theory to help you understand how most people and organizations make decisions and how you can learn to make better decisions.

As we've noted previously, decision making is a skill that can improve with practice. Many people make decisions based on intuition—they follow their gut. But while effective business professionals don't ignore their instincts, they make evidence-based decisions based on critical thinking. Listening and fact gathering are important parts of this process.

Shrewd business professionals try to make measured decisions based on rational thinking, and they try to avoid rash or impulsive judgments whenever possible. A quick decision is not usually a correct decision.

You Don't Have to Be Perfect: Bounded Rationality and Decision Making

Bounded rationality is a term coined by Herbert Simon (1916–2001), a multidisciplinary educator ahead of his time, to describe the way that groups make decisions. Bounded rationality rejects the long-established maximization theory of decision making in favor of optimization. This theory looks at group decisions with multiple goals and various stakeholders, a worldview paradigm that includes the types of decisions complex organizations face.

Simon studied how people process limited available information with imperfect logic, leading to the concept of bounded rationality. He created the term *satisficing* to define how individuals and organizations achieve the perceived best position in decisions while relying on imperfect or incomplete information.

Simon's theory builds on John Nash's game theory by defining the optimal group decision as *satisficing*. Some in the group are satisfied, while some are merely accepting of the decision as "good enough." Satisficing takes into account the relative importance of the decision for each stakeholder.

Herbert Simon contributed vast insight into problem solving and the decision-making process across academic fields by applying principles of sociology, psychology, management science, economics, political science, and philosophy. Simon correctly predicted that the public sector role in decision making would increase in impact, adding complexity to social problem resolution and decision making. The ethics of concepts like environmentalism or improved lifestyle were unquantifiable, unmeasurable, and, as a result, uncertain.

Simon rejected the classical economic assumption of perfect knowledge in these types of decisions and derived *bounded rationality* to better describe decision making in the face of uncertainty. According to Simon, *how* decisions are made better indicates real-world conditions of resource allocation than *what* decisions are made.

In methodology, Simon preferred a blend of academic thought experiments, laboratory work, and empirical observations of thinking and decision making to the sterile "think-tank" environment. According to Simon, human rationality is bounded externally by social constraints and internally by cognitive restraints; conformity and possibility are unquantifiable constraints in the process. In Simon's theory, quantification is used to enhance rationality, not create it. When management sets conditions for rational thought, some actions are predisposed to be viewed as nonworking solutions.

Common sense, or heuristics, applies metrics as a screening tool. Human perception and rationality are both bounded—perfect knowledge is not possible in complex decisions with multiple stakeholders. Quantitative results assume the status of powerful symbols, a talisman that may be imperfectly understood, but is nevertheless used to justify decisions. Managers may experience numbers as symbolic guidance with technical rationality, capacity to quantify. Economic, social, legal, and political stakeholders, although largely invisible throughout the process, impact the final decision, limiting the number of reasonable solutions.

Simon understood that complex problems break down into hierarchies, systems of considering means and ends to reach decisions. Applying rationality, perfect information does not exist. Decision-making processes are iterative. The rational way to decide is to choose a solution, try it out, and fix those problems created by the decision.

In the real world, perfect decisions are mythical. Managers decide through satisficing, with a goal of being as optimal as the competition rather than as optimal as possible. Optimization costs more than the marginal income generated by reaching it. In other words, perfection is the enemy of the very good, and in business, it is generally enough to be very good. You don't have to be perfect.

Simon's next contribution to the problem of decision making was formulating design theory. According to Simon, creative thinkers clearly formulate the problem *first*. Problems are unfamiliar and poorly defined situations. Resolving problems involves two possible decisions:

- Pick from a list of goods or services that already exist.
- Create something unique.

In either case, successful resolution is not controlled by the problem solver/decision maker. Choosing among the existing is convention, conformity. Successfully creating something unique depends on the reaction of the intended audience. The irony is that, as we have noted previously, problem solving and decision making are skills, and skills require practice.

Subjective expected utility (SEU), the traditional unit of measurement for the soundness of decisions, is a quantitative look, not at statistical-driven decisions but at perfect-knowledge decisions. The SEU theory translates poorly in actual laboratory testing of game theories. People actually tend to satisfice and then react with vengeance against those who cross them.

Another weakness in SEU theory is that the way a problem is presented affects the decision-making process. This problem has been described by Nobel Prize–winning behavioral economists Daniel Kahneman and Amos Tversky as *framing*. Kahneman and Tversky found that people made different decisions depending on how a problem was presented to them, even when the outcome of the decision was the same.

In Kahneman and Tverksy's experiment, subjects were presented with two possible solutions for six hundred people affected with a deadly virus. Choice A will save two hundred lives, while choice B has a 33% chance of saving all six hundred lives and a 66% chance of saving no one. While the expected value of two hundred lives is the same in both scenarios, three out of four respondents selected choice A.

Here's where the experiment gets interesting. Kahneman and Tversky presented the exact same statistical outcomes to a second group of subjects, but they framed the problem differently. This time, choice C would cause four hundred people to die, while choice D had a 33% chance that no one would die and a 66% chance that everyone would die. When the problem was framed this way, the outcomes were reversed. Three out of four respondents chose the second option, *even though choice B and choice D have identical outcomes!*

What Kahneman and Tversky showed is that how you frame a problem has a real impact on how people behave in solving the problem. Similarly, the credit card industry argued over whether price differences should be called "cash discounts" or "credit surcharges." The statements have equivalent real effects; however, psychological legitimacy was at stake. Are credit card purchases the normal condition or is paying cash? The industry determined that people were more likely to pay with cash when an increased price was defined as a "credit surcharge" than when it was described as a "cash discount."

In his analysis of human behavior in management, Simon found the administrative decision breaks down into two major components:

- Cost Element: Budget drives potential solutions before the problem is even framed.
- Results of Resolution: This element is complex as it relates to the goals envisaged by the decision maker and how the problem is framed, whether these goals conflict with personal goals, public service, or for-profit public service. Is the resolution in harmony with the policy and the mission of the organization? The administrative decision cannot be rational 100% of the time. The director must be satisfied with solutions that are acceptable rather than optimal.

The growing field of Operational Research and Management Science offers these tools to help business professionals improve their decision-making skills:

- Optimality: Scheduling procedures, such as Gantt charts or program analysis and review technique (PERT), which combine common sense inputs and mathematical logic to create gaming scenarios and to advance management preparedness to make decisions. These tools can also be used to define problems.
- Experiments on Decision Making: You can assess your organizational behavior and institutional "think" by creating internal measurements on how decisions are made.
- Persuasion and Evocation: The process varies inputs of premises and assesses outputs of conclusions. The

output at each step of the process serves as the input for the next step. Persuasion, then, begins with selecting inputs. Conflicting inputs are not rare. This research questions the motivation to participate in inputs. Does the conscious selection of inputs steer a decision toward a personal goal? A corporate goal?

- The Structure of Decisions: Systemized common sense refers to behavior and choice within an organization, so conformity to organizational norms is itself an input. Is computerization a tool of this conformity? Or, at the very least, is it standardization of potential solutions?

Simon's research advocates an intentional worldview approach to business professionalism. Be aware of differing or competing agendas, problem-framing opportunities, and institutional conformity that discourages innovation and creative problem solving. Stay abreast of current research in decision making and problem solving. As you learn to satisfice, you will improve your decision-making efficiency and effectiveness.

Summary

In this chapter, we have explored concepts associated with our second pillar: professional self-management. By acting like a professional, managing resources effectively, engaging in periodic self-assessment, and learning to make "good enough" decisions, you will enhance your reputation and abilities as a business professional. In our assertiveness model, you will want to decide whether you are a dolphin or a minnow. And you'll want to stop swimming with sharks.

The next chapter will focus on the third pillar: professional presence or image.

Further Reading

Gigerenzer, Gerd and Selten, Reinhard. *Bounded Rationality*. Cambridge: MIT Press, 2002.

Kahneman, Daniel. "Maps of Bounded Rationality: Psychology for Behavioral Economics." *The American Economic Review*, 93, no. 5, 2003, 1449–75.

Kahneman, Daniel., Diener, Ed., & Schwarz, Norbert (eds). *Well-Being: The Foundations of Hedonic Psychology*. New York: Russell Sage Foundation, 2003.

Project Management Institute. *A Guide to the Project Management Body Of Knowledge (3rd ed. ed.)*. Project Management Institute, 2003.

Simon, Herbert. "A Behavioral Model of Rational Choice," in *Models of Man, Social and Rational: Mathematical Essays on Rational Human Behavior in a Social Setting*. New York: Wiley, 1957.

Case Study One

Gwen is a thirty-five-year-old experienced administrative assistant at a large insurance company in a city of one hundred thousand people. She is married and has children, but her family is at a good time and place to consider relocation. Gwen recently completed a Bachelor's degree in organizational leadership through an online adult degree completion program.

Gwen is considered to be organized and responsible by others, including her managers. Her current organization has several jobs that require degrees that are open for applications. But Gwen is afraid she will not be respected by others in the company because she started out as a mail clerk. She thinks she should seek employment elsewhere. She has trouble seeing herself as a peer to her former managers.

Imagine that you are a career coach who is meeting with Gwen. Is Gwen a dolphin, a minnow, or a shark? What action steps from Chapters 3 and 4 would you suggest to Gwen?

⁓❦ **EXERCISE ONE** ❦⁓

Considering the assertiveness model in Chapter Four, are you a dolphin, a minnow, or a shark? Are you comfortable with your assertiveness? Use Appendix E as a resource in your assessment. What are some professional self-management considerations to examine as you define your assertiveness?

Case Study Two

Roz and Carolyn are walking buddies at work. Roz is a bright, energetic, hardworking woman. She is also a self-described "emotional hothead" who has recently reentered the workforce after raising a child. Carolyn is a veteran, mature, even-keeled professional. Things have changed in terms of culture, technology, and the world of work during the twelve years Roz was out of the workforce. Roz would like Carolyn to work with her as a paid career coach with a two-hour session on Saturday afternoon. Carolyn has asked you, as a senior business coach, to help her put together a lesson plan.

Develop a one-afternoon business professionalism workshop from material you have read in this book so far. What agenda would you recommend for Carolyn? Based on what you have learned so far, what are the most important areas Roz should focus on as she reintegrates into the workplace?

❧ EXERCISE TWO ❧

Create a self-management SWOT (strengths, weaknesses, opportunities, and threats) analysis. How can you capitalize on your strengths to create opportunities and manage threats? What can you do to mitigate your weaknesses?

❧ EXERCISE THREE ❧

Write your answers to the following questions. Writing helps to commit the answer in your mind.

- What is/will be your profession?
- What are the knowledge requirements?
- How do you manage your time?
- How do you make decisions?
- How important are ethical decisions and self-discipline within your working environment?

Action Plan
See Appendix B.

There are three levels of assessment/evaluation to help assess your assertiveness. Choose honest people who give good feedback.

Individual
See Appendix G. Reflective practice based on core principles.

Master/Peer Assessment
See Appendix H. Requested from a trusted advisor/mentor/peer.

360-Degree Assessment
See Appendix I. Requested from key trusted people around you.

CHAPTER 5

Pillar Three: Professional Presence/Image

Rob has always possessed a laid-back personality. And he maintains that relaxed, easygoing persona at work. He has been with his current organization for six years. In that period, Rob has applied for several management positions for which he believes he is well qualified. But each time, he is passed over for promotion in favor of a "go-getter." What actions can Rob take to create a professional presence that is more likely to be considered management material?

I am a member of the baby boom generation. The professional image mantra that was drilled into boomers' heads was simple and powerful: "You can always dress up, but you cannot dress down." The message in that bon mot concerns the importance of first impressions on how you will be judged by superiors and peers. Appearances matter. Like it or not, you will be sized up by your appearance. In my demographic, you are what you wear, and given the strong religious and corporate influence in the age of IBM and Madison Avenue, what you wore was a white-collared shirt, a dark suit, and a conservatively tasteful necktie. Women had a bit more latitude in their professional dress, but not much: in the seventies, a woman in a pantsuit was making a political statement whether she meant to or not.

As boomers like me are beginning to retire, some are becoming increasingly more casual in both their dress and their professional demeanor. Generations X and Y have continued and even accelerated the "dress down" trend both in the workplace/marketplace and in their social spheres. Black tie and jacket dress is reserved for very formal occasions, if at all—in Idaho, where I live, people wear their "dress jeans" and fanciest belt buckles to formal social events.

Today, even some banks, once bastions of professional conservatism, are adopting business casual dress codes. And the technology sector, dominated by Generations X and Y, has made casual clothing the uniform of the early twenty-first century.

But, culturally, some international and US regional areas have remained relatively formal due to traditional cultural and religious forms and forces. I believe that the boomer mantra still has important applications in today's increasingly casual society.

In Chapter One, we briefly explored the ideas of choices and constraints, individualism and purpose, and self and the community. In this chapter, we will expand on those concepts to develop the third pillar of our business professionalism core: professional image/presence.

Every business professional should develop a core set of knowledge, skills, attitudes, and behaviors that guide their practice, including a businesslike mindset or judgment in terms of appropriate and enlightened self-interest; that means ethics and appropriate personal norms and standards. These core elements should form their professional worldview in terms of presence/image.

In the early twenty-first century, what are the acceptable standards of appearance, presence, and image for the effective business professional?

Appearance

For older generations, formality still matters. Dressing up for formal events and demonstrating clothing and manners appropriate to the situation was important for the generation whose careers blossomed in the post-WWII years. People were absolutely judged by their appearances, not to mention their knowledge and use of complex tableware settings. Lessons in etiquette formed an important part of every young professional's development.

Today, "status dressing" would seem to be diminished in importance. Business professional dress seems to be more situational and casual. But is it really? Or have the symbols of status merely shifted to new icons?

I believe that now more than ever, business professionals need to look at the concept of developing a professional core in terms of presence and image. A business professional employed with a company in the 1950s could expect to spend his or her entire professional career with a single organization. Not so today, when people change jobs and even careers as casually as they have changed their professional dress standards.

Professional image and presence is perhaps even more important now than it was in the past for one simple reason: your professional image defines your personal brand. And every business professional should be actively engaged in creating a persona that reflects a desirable brand to the marketplace. Whether you know it or not, your career probably depends on your ability to craft a desirable, trustworthy, and engaging professional image.

Attitude/Confidence

Do you have a theme song? You should. A Gen X friend of mine loves the song "Short Skirt, Long Jacket" by the alternative band Cake. Whenever she walks into a meeting or is about to give a presentation, she mentally cues that song. The horns, the beat, and the inspiring lyrics ("She's touring the facilities and cutting through red tape") give her a spring in her step and a sparkle in her eye—the signs of a confident and accomplished business professional.

As business professionals develop and mature in their experience and ability, they should develop an attendant sense of confidence and competence. If you don't feel confident, fake it until you do. Confidence is a practiced attitude and behavior. Like every other part of professionalism, confidence should be an intentional part of the professional core, requiring both practice and reflection.

Remember, though, that you never want healthy confidence to be confused with unhealthy or narcissistic arrogance. A confident professional believes in his or her abilities and feels comfortable with his or her peers.

Social Norms/Roles

What are the rules and social norms at your workplace? Is your organization more formal, with rigidly defined hierarchical reporting structures? Or is it more informal and open?

Effective business professionals make an effort to know and respect social norms and rules in their organizations, associations, and/or communities. If you can't articulate the rules and social norms at your organization, then you have some homework. Knowledge of social norms and rules should be considered as a part of the professional core in terms of practice and decision making.

Socialization Process

As part of their personal development plan and professional core, business professionals should actively participate in social engagements including work parties, association meetings, and community events. Before and after any social engagements, effective business professionals should consider their core standards of behavior, and after the events, they should assess their effectiveness using reflective practice.

A note on drinking at work parties: know your tolerance for alcohol. If it's no more than two drinks, have one. If one drink loosens your tongue too much, stick with seltzer water. Or designate yourself as a driver. You'll be a hero to your co-workers, and you may save yourself from an uncomfortable situation. You are still "on the job" at social occasions—you represent your organization. And more importantly, you represent yourself.

Traits/Genetics/Environment

Effective business professionals are aware that there are certain personal traits, genetics, and environmental constraints that affect professional presence or image.

What do I mean? Well, consider this statistic: in 2005, a survey of Fortune 500 company CEOs revealed that their average height was six feet, more than two inches taller than the average American male. This finding was consistent with earlier research about leadership and height.

Does this mean that if you are shorter than six feet, or if you are a woman, you can't be the CEO of a Fortune 500 company? Of course not. But it does indicate what many social scientists already know—we tend to judge people by their appearances. Malcolm Gladwell calls this type of leadership bias "The Warren G. Harding Principle" in *Blink*, his 2007 book on the power and prevalence of instinctive decision making. Warren G. Harding was by most accounts a terrible president. But he *looked* presidential, so people voted for him.

Knowing which traits and environmental circumstances can be unfavorable to you will help you to turn personal weaknesses into strengths. As you engage in reflective practice in interpersonal and social situations, aim to identify possible issues with your professional image and devise framing strategies to deal proactively with things beyond your control. For example, if you happen to be a short leader, make that a strength and a selling point. Most CEOs are tall. So your height makes you truly extraordinary and individual. It helps you to stand out from the crowd.

Building the Brand That Is You

I mentioned at the beginning of this chapter that your professional image is essentially your personal brand. You should put as much care and thought into your appearance as you would into marketing a new product or service. The following are all considerations as you shape your unique professional image:

- Is my organizational culture conservative or liberal?
- Does my profession value good manners and social skills?

- What is my organization's official dress code? How closely is this dress code followed?
- What is the average age of midlevel managers at my organization? Are most of them baby boomers? Or are most Gen Xers?
- What are my most attractive features, and what can I do to highlight them in a work-appropriate manner?
- What can I do to maintain a healthy physical appearance?
- What subtle wardrobe accessories can I use to enhance my personal brand?
- Can I explain who I am and what I do in a thirty-second elevator pitch? Is my pitch compelling enough to convince the person who hears it to get off at my floor and continue the conversation?

As you consider the answers to these questions, you will create a professional image that reflects the real you: confident, professional, and unique.

A Final Note: The Job Interview

When you are interviewing for a job, the baby boomer mantra will serve you well. A job interview is not the time to make a statement about your personal image. Research the organization, its culture, and its dress code as closely as possible. If you can, talk to current employees. Then dress at least one step up from the level you identify. For men or women, a navy blue or gray suit is always a safe choice. Women should avoid excessive makeup and flashy jewelry. Men should choose conservative neckties. In business, taking the time to dress up for an interview shows that you really care about the position and that you are willing to take extra steps to demonstrate that commitment.

And as you walk in, cue the mental theme song and stand tall. Confidence is a key to success.

Summary

Professional image and presence is how you make an impression in the business community. Study the norms and conventions of your specific profession, and do not challenge them. Your physical appearance should reflect your career goals. Know your organization's and industry's culture. Invest in your wardrobe and maintain your physical health. Developing a confident attitude is important to your success.

Now that we've covered the first three pillars—professional formation, self-management, and professional image—we are ready to tackle the number one source of trouble and strife in the workplace.

The next chapter will focus on the fourth pillar of a business professional's core: professional communication.

Further Reading

Cardon, Peter W. and Okoro, Ephraim A. "Focus on Business Practices: Professional Characteristics Communicated by Formal Versus Casual Workplace Attire." *Business Communication Quarterly* 72 (2009), 355.

Gladwell, Malcolm. *Blink: The Power of Thinking without Thinking*. New York: Little, Brown and Company, 2005.

Gunn, Tim and Moloney, Kate. *Tim Gunn: A Guide to Quality, Taste, and Style.* New York: Abrams Image, 2007.

Peluchette, Joy V. and Karl, Katherine. "The impact of workplace attire on employee self-perceptions." *Human Resource Development Quarterly* 18, no.3 (2007), 345-360.

Case Study

You were part of a small group of employees at a small credit union branch office who approached the CEO during an open-door policy session and took her up on a chance to provide operational feedback. The small group voiced to her that some of the staff were too casual in their appearance and behavior. The CEO agreed and asked you to set up a two-hour, brown bag training session on staff professional image and presence.

Write a brief outline of the agenda for the event.

∞ EXERCISE ∞

Take stock of your professional image/presence. You may want to use some of the questions in this chapter to assess how well you have developed your personal brand. Are you projecting the image that you want to project? How can you improve?

Application Exercise

- What is your business presence/image?
- What is it about your professional presence that attracts customers to your business?
- What are the business implications of cultural orientation under business professionalism?
- Have you created both a business-related and a personal one-minute elevator speech? Practice it.

Action Plan
See Appendix C.

CHAPTER 6

Pillar Four: Professional Communication

Tim's preferred form of work communication is to send e-mails. He has developed a reputation for e-mailing even simple greetings and sending nonwork related notes to co-workers in cubicles next to his, rather than saying hello or making small talk. Tim likes the informal nature of e-mail. He says things in e-mails he would never say in person.

What is one of the biggest barriers to productivity in the workplace? sWhat hurts morale, creates legal problems, and potentially damages the reputations of organizations and individuals? Professional communication is one of the basic functions of management, and it is the fourth pillar of the business professionalism core. The ability to communicate effectively is what will truly set you apart from your peers.

It is commonly accepted that effective and professional communication is one of the biggest challenges in business practice. Even though every job description from shift manager at a fast food restaurant to CEO requires "excellent written and verbal communication skills," surveys of business practitioners have named poor communication as the number one problem facing businesses and organizations. In fact, a 2011 longitudinal survey of college effectiveness in teaching written communication skills showed that an astonishing 44% of students from four-year universities graduated with no discernible improvement in their writing abilities.

Couple the woeful lack of academic preparation for effective organizational communication with globalization and the rapid rise of technological innovations, and you have a recipe for disaster. Indeed, most organizations face myriad challenges in managing and monitoring their company messages, both internal and external.

Like the other principles we have discussed, professional communication is a skill that can be acquired and improved on. You may not have learned the things you needed in your college classroom, but you can learn to craft a message that is succinct and effective. Professional communication is an integral part of a business professional's core principles.

Audience and Purpose

All effective communication starts with identifying these two concepts: Who is my audience? What is my purpose? Your medium of communication—e-mail, phone call, individual or group meeting, or formal memo—depends on your answer to these two questions.

Audience considerations include:
Internal or External: Your tone and the amount of information you convey often depend on whether your communication is to someone within your organization or outside of it. If you are

communicating with a regulatory agency, for example, you will want to adopt a high level of formality and should probably seek approval before you send your message.

Organizational Hierarchy: Are you communicating with subordinates or superiors? Your level of formality, as well as the medium you choose, depends on the level of hierarchy.

High Context vs. Low Context: Diversity adds a wealth of experience and understanding to organizations, but it can also create communication barriers. Knowing whether your audience comes from a high context (such as Japan or China) or low context (the United States) culture will help you to craft an effective message, especially with respect to your gestures and nonverbal communication.

Your purpose also determines your medium and tone. Are you writing an informal email response to a routine question? Or are you preparing an annual report to present to senior management? Are you creating a marketing presentation, or an informational training session? Your purpose will drive the way you organize and communicate your message.

Once you have identified your audience and purpose, you can choose the appropriate delivery method for your message.

Medium—Oral or Written?

A friend of mine who had spent several years as part of the legal team for Royal Dutch Shell once gave me some invaluable advice: "Never put anything in writing that you might regret later."

Effective business professionals know when things should be documented and how they should be documented. Make sure you know your company's policy about documentation and that you follow it. Deciding upon the appropriate form—oral or written—can be critical to your message's success. The classic legal case of

Pearson v. Post, in which two parties entered into a shipping contract without actually agreeing on the ship that would be used, illustrates that in many documents and words, there is considerable opportunity for errors and misunderstandings.

An important note: if you're like Tim, and think that e-mail is a good tool for idle chitchat or for saying things to people that you would never say in person, think again. E-mail is forever. Each and every e-mail you send creates a permanent and legally discoverable record. What do you want your permanent record to say about you?

Some activities require written documentation. Keep meeting notes, including any agreements or promises, whether you or your associates made them. Immediately memorialize these notes in memos to the appropriate people and follow up on progress and action items in e-mail. Your reputation as a thorough and effective professional will be enhanced as you honor promises and expect others to do the same.

Clarity and Conciseness

The seventeenth-century French mathematician Blaise Pascal once famously wrote, "Please excuse the length of my letter. I had no time to write a short one." Indeed, being concise often takes more work than writing *War and Peace*. But the extra effort is worth it.

The first rule of effective business communication is this: eschew obfuscation. If you have no idea what that phrase means, you're not alone. Let's put it a different way: don't use big words when small ones will do better. Business professionals should strive for clarity in verbal and written communications. That means developing a concise and action-oriented writing style rather than the long-winded, SAT vocabulary–laced passages that your college professors probably encouraged.

I once had a colleague who was known for sending two-thousand-word e-mails. While he could not be accused of not covering all his bases, none of us had time to read through the flowery salutations and flattery to get to the meat of the message. Several people had politely tried to hint that this gentleman should adopt a more concise e-mail style. Finally, one colleague sat down with him, printed out his most recent missive, and used a Sharpie pen to scratch out 90% of what he had written. The remaining 10% is what he should have sent.

Ground Rules

If you want to communicate effectively with other members of an organization, set your ground rules early. Effective business professionals, set up situationally appropriate ground rules in conversations and meetings to ensure that time is used well and goals and objectives are met. The ground rules must be appropriate to the situation and agreed upon by all parties in order for this practice to succeed.

Discernment/Judgment

An old proverb states, "When a man is silent, others consider him profound even though he is a fool." Shrewd business professionals know when to speak and when to remain quiet. They also know how much or how little to say in each situation. As a rule of thumb, God wisely gave you two ears and one mouth. Use them in that proportion.

Evaluation

A skill every business professional should develop is the ability to evaluate the quality and worth of a document or oral presentation. The ability to assess the quality of one's own work and critique the communications of others is crucial. This critical thinking process is developed along a learning curve and will be improved by reflective practice.

Take the opportunity to observe and evaluate master communicators whenever possible. You might consider joining a local forum group or an organization like Toastmasters, where you will have the chance to observe several speakers and presenters for effectiveness. Note what works for you in these presentations and what doesn't. Then incorporate your observations into your own presentations. We learn by observation and frequent practice.

Arguments

Effective business professionals have the ability to build cases for and/or against positions. This skill is improved by reflective practice. There are several books on rhetoric that will improve your ability to make effective arguments. You should learn which argument style will be most effective for your case. For example, you may want to use the Aristotelian classical style of argument, which moves from general inferences to a specific conclusion. Or you may want to try Rogerian argumentation, which considers and defuses objections to your position up front and attempts to find common ground.

Internally, get into the habit of playing the devil's advocate. Argue for your position and then argue against it. This practice may help you understand your opponent's view. If you understand their view, you can explain and potentially defend your view more effectively. Always anticipate the potential arguments against your position, and attempt to defuse them early.

Negotiation

Entire books have been written about the art of negotiation. The art and science of negotiations is a skill developed through practice and experience. In general, negotiations end with a compromise, which some wits have described as a situation where no one leaves the table with what they want.

Successful negotiation requires that you decide what you want to achieve and what it is worth to achieve it before you even sit down at the table. What do you have to achieve? What are you willing to concede? Negotiation requires that you rank your values. Avoid situations of urgency or circumstances where personal favors confuse and misdirect.

And work on your poker face. You don't want to give the game away.

Relationships

The power of relationships in business cannot be understated. Effective business professionals build relationships through interpersonal and social communications. Those relationships are intentionally nurtured. Sincerely caring about your associates refreshes your spirit and broadens your existence. In more pragmatic terms, knowing the right people and being able to call on them also helps you to get your job done.

The power of a simple thank-you note (handwritten or e-mailed, depending on the level of the favor) cannot be denied. Get in the habit of building relationships and nurturing them through frequent and sincere communication.

Presentations

It has been famously said that more Americans are afraid of public speaking than of death, which means that the average person would rather be in the casket than delivering the eulogy. Public speaking is an art—in fact, the term *rhetoric* was developed in Ancient Greece to describe the art of speaking. Like any skill, speaking should be practiced. Delivering an important presentation cold can set you up for failure.

If and when you are asked to make a presentation, you will likely need to use a form of professional presentation software. The dominant presentation tool is, of course, PowerPoint, though new competitors like Prezi are promising to spice up the conventional ten slide presentation format.

In general, PowerPoints should be simple and direct. They should never be your presentation—you, as the presenter, should use your PowerPoint as a visual to enhance your message. Too often, PowerPoints detract from the message with distracting or confusing visuals, or too much text, leading to the moniker, "death by PowerPoint." For advice on how to create a memorable presentation, read Chip and Dan Heath's *Made to Stick: Why Some Ideas Survive and Others Die*.

Plan ahead and know what technology will be available. Prepare printed versions of your presentation in case the technology malfunctions. And don't let a technological malfunction shake you from your message. As a speaker, talk slowly and clearly. Pause to let major points sink in. Allow time for questions at the end of your presentation.

The more you practice presenting to groups, the more comfortable you will become. Again, you might consider joining an organization like Toastmasters, where you can both observe and be observed.

Technology

Remember the example of Tim? He illustrates why technology is both a blessing and curse to the business professional. Technology, like any other business tool, should be used to increase productivity, to organize, and to effectively communicate. It should not be used excessively and inappropriately when communicating interpersonally or socially. The faceless, transient feeling of e-mail sometimes allows people to make critical errors of judgment.

Here are a few technology dos and don'ts for organizations.

Do

- Use e-mail for calendaring and for announcements.
- Create shared virtual workspaces where colleagues can collaborate.
- Encourage the use of WebEx and other video conferencing tools to save on travel costs.

Don't

- Use e-mail for emotional conversations. There is no substitute for a face-to-face meeting in potentially confrontational situations.
- Use social media on company time, unless you are explicitly engaged in activities designed to build networks or promote your organization.
- Use text messaging as a substitute for a phone call. In fact, you may want to create an organizational or personal communication policy that avoids the use of texts or instant messages entirely.

Elevator Pitch

As we've discussed in previous chapters, business professionals should have a core set of principles and a well-thought-out worldview. This worldview should be presented in the form of a well-developed and rehearsed elevator pitch. An elevator pitch is basically the one minute sales pitch for the brand that is you. When and if the opportunity presents itself, business professionals should be able to communicate their worldview in an engaging, convincing, situationally appropriate manner.

Summary

In this chapter, we have covered some of the promises and pitfalls of organizational communication. The ability to communicate your ideas effectively, both orally and in writing, will set you apart from other business professionals and enable you to achieve your goals. Like all skills, communication takes practice, and colleges have not adequately prepared students for the demands of the business world. Take opportunities to observe others and to practice your skills. Be mindful at all times of your audience and purpose, and choose your communication medium appropriately.

Now that we have learned the Four Pillars of business professionalism, we are ready to look at potential applications of these pillars in the business world.

Further Reading

Gerson, Sharon J. Gerson, Steven M. *Workplace Communication: Process and Product*. Upper Saddle River, NJ: Pearson Prentice Hall, 2007.

Goleman, Daniel, *Emotional Intelligence*, New York: Bantam, 1997.

Senge, Peter M. *The Fifth Discipline: The Art and Practice of the Learning Organization*. New York: Doubleday, 1990.

Aristotle, *The Art of Rhetoric*.

Arum, Richard and Roksa, Josipa. *Academically Adrift: Limited Learning on College Campus*. Chicago: University of Chicago Press, 2010.

Heath, Chip and Heath, Dan. *Made to Stick: Why Some Ideas Survive and Others Die*. New York: Random House, 2007.

Toulmin, Stephen. *The Uses of Argument*. Cambridge: Cambridge University Press, 1958.

Case Study

The principal at Whitney Elementary has often complained that his teachers are so busy doing tasks that they neglect basic professional communications skills. He has accepted your bid as a business coach to conduct a one-day in-service on the topic of business communications. The teachers are doing a good job of teaching and doing administrative tasks, but they have issues effectively communicating with administrators, the community, and parents.

Based on what you have learned in this chapter, write an agenda for the one-day in-service that addresses the teachers' need for improved professional communication.

∽ EXERCISE ∾

Everyone can probably identify "the work e-mail I wish I hadn't sent." Can you think of one? What does this e-mail say about your communication style? Write down five strengths in your current practice. Now write down five areas where you need to improve.

Application Exercise

Craft a one-minute elevator pitch for a potential job inquiry, explaining your skills and identifying your world view. Your pitch should be no more than one page, double spaced (250 words) in length.

Action Plan
See Appendix D.

CHAPTER 7

Applying the Four Pillars

Sally is a thirty-five-year-old midcareer professional. She has plateaued in her current sales representative role and feels she is ready for new challenges and responsibilities. Sally has been asked to apply for an internal management training program next year. What can she do now to prepare for the training program?

The Four Pillars are not business professionalism—they are the supports that aid a business professional in achieving an effective, productive, happy career. Where are you today in your own career? Are you just starting out? Are you a seasoned veteran who chuckled knowingly as you read some of the examples in previous chapters? Or are you a midlevel professional like Sally, ready for more challenges but unsure how to reach the next level?

Application of each pillar is role specific—in other words, you have to adapt the principle to fit your personal needs. But business professionalism core principles apply to all levels of employees. As you apply the Four Pillars to your work habits and goals, you will see changes, some slow, some more immediate. What are you waiting for?

No matter where you are in your current career, you can start applying the principles today. But change requires commitment. Now is the time for you to:

1. Accept responsibility for your personal and professional development.
2. Express enthusiasm and passion for life. Either find your dream job or start dreaming about the one you already have, but do not wait until later to become more professional.
3. Seek a mentor who can model the business professionalism behaviors and who can provide support, coaching, and networking.
4. Teach what you have learned to others. The act of teaching is itself a powerful way to learn and apply principles.

As I mentioned, how you apply the Four Pillars depends on where you currently are in your career. Let's look at some examples.

Leaders/Managers/Supervisors

This level of application is usually reserved for masters and upper journeymen. It requires a high degree of familiarity with the Four Pillars and a lifelong commitment to business professionalism that can inspire others.

Business professionals who exercise authority over other employees or who motivate and influence other employees are theoretically responsible not only for the classical functions of management—planning, leading, organizing, and controlling—but they are also responsible for guiding their subordinates' development and growth. If planned strategically and proactively, that employee growth and development will be an investment in future business professional performance.

Too often, senior management waits for a crisis. The need to act with urgency often undercuts management's ability to act professionally and ethically. Consider the example of British Petroleum's 2010 catastrophic oil spill in the Gulf of Mexico. The company's senior management was widely considered to be unprepared and unprofessional in its response to the crisis. Rather than accepting responsibility and trying to solve the problem, BP management lost several critical days trying to avoid accountability. At the end of the day, when the CEO finally apologized, "I'm sorry" just wasn't enough.

Contrast British Petroleum's junior-high-school behavior with Johnson and Johnson's now legendary 1982 response to tampering with Tylenol packages. The company exemplified the pillars of business professionalism in its swift and comprehensive response. They initiated an immediate nationwide recall of the product and cooperated with all authorities to investigate the tampering and to design ways to ensure the problem could never happen again. While the recall affected immediate short-term profits, Johnson and Johnson's ethics-based response prevented future deaths. It also translated into a long-term win for the Tylenol brand.

Business professionals with leadership or management responsibilities should use the pillar model in planning professional development for their subordinates and for themselves. It is also important for them to understand the assertiveness model and practice dolphinlike behaviors. Finally, they should implement the development model, creating an organization where professionals at all levels can learn skills from each other to become more effective, productive, and happy.

Employees

Even if you are not a manager and don't want to be one, you still have the responsibility to behave like a business professional.

Business professionals with nonsupervisory responsibilities should also use the pillar model, understand the assertiveness process, and implement the development model to be effective. If done correctly, that growth and development will be an investment in future business professional performance. Technicians and paraprofessionals will benefit as well.

Implementing the pillar model will earn you the trust and respect of your peers and supervisors. It will enable you to accomplish your work more quickly and with fewer of the inevitable "bumps" that seem to creep onto every business project's road. As you model the Four Pillars, you will find that your work day is calm and productive. You may notice that your managers give more desirable, challenging, or interesting tasks to you. They will recognize your professionalism and reward it.

Independent Contractors

If you work for yourself, the business professionalism model I've presented probably feels familiar to you, because your success depends on your reputation for being honest, fair, and for meeting deadlines and communicating effectively.

Self-employed business professionals may lack the structure of formal organizations, but they should also use the pillar model, understand the assertiveness process, and implement the development model to be effective. If done correctly, that growth and development will be an investment in future business professional performance.

Your business professionalism should be a hallmark of your brand. If you are known for professionalism, people will want to work with you. Since you probably won't find them within your work, look for mentoring relationships through community or professional organizations. If you are just starting out, a mentor can help you with everything from the practical (starting your own LLC, filing tax returns) to the ephemeral (building connections in the community).

Building the Pillars into Your Organization

Business professionalism doesn't happen by accident. It takes careful planning, skill-building, and self-assessment. The following are some suggestions for how an organization might use the Four Pillars:

1. Create an institutional mentoring program that matches more senior journeymen or masters with apprentices.
2. Do a company-wide 360 assessment to identify areas of potential growth and improvement.
3. Incorporate the Four Pillars into policy documents. For example, develop a communications policy that focuses on audience, purpose, and mediums.
4. Write and enforce a dress code that reflects the underlying mission and values of your organization.
5. Make self-assessment and self-management a part of annual performance reviews.
6. Create an organizational culture that expects and rewards business professionalism.

Summary

Application of the Four Pillars depends on your current role and on your desired role in your organization. As you practice business professionalism, your reputation will improve, and you will find that you are happier, more productive, and more effective in your work.

So what advice would you give to Sally about how she can take her career to the next level? What advice would you give to yourself? And most importantly, what are you waiting for? The right time to apply the Four Pillars is today and every day.

If you wait for someone else to direct your professional development or your career, you may wait forever. Take charge of your professional development today by planning to implement the Four Pillars in your life.

Further Reading

Bennis, Warren G., Parikh, Jagdish, and Lessem, Ronnie, *Beyond Leadership: Balancing Economics, Ethics and Ecology*, Blackwell Publishers, 1994.

Fink, Steven. *Crisis Management: Planning for the Inevitable*. Lincoln, NE: iUniverse, 2000.

Kouzes, James and Posner, Barry. *The Leadership Challenge*. San Francisco: Jossey-Bass, 2008.

Case Study

You are an independent business consultant who specializes in risk management. You are contacted by a local start-up software firm and asked to draft a crisis management plan. With the Four Pillars—professional formation, self-management, presence and image, and communication—in mind, create a questionnaire to assess the current mindset of the company's management.

❦ EXERCISE ❦

Think about these issues with respect to your current role in your organization:

- Decision making and problem solving are skills, not tools. Practice skills to become more talented in these areas. By making decisions, even if they are not implemented, you can compare them with the actual decision or problem solution. How can you sharpen your decision-making skills?
- Question your institutional structure. How would you describe the organization's communication channels? Are possible solutions limited? Do computerization and standardization lead to conformity? Can you or should you work to change the system?
- Write down one specific, concrete goal for implementing one of the Four Pillars into your daily routine. Perhaps you need to work on your communication. Or maybe self-management is an issue for you. Choose one area, and describe your plans for improvement. If applicable, share those plans with your supervisor and solicit his or her feedback.

CHAPTER 8

The Future of Business Professionalism

Bill is a forty-year-old veteran worker in the insurance industry. He has worked his way up from telemarketing to claims management as a supervisor. He has seen and survived several corporate downsizing episodes during his fifteen-year tenure at the firm. What steps could Bill take in terms of professional development to help ensure he continues to survive future layoffs?

No one can predict the future. But a business professional's survival may depend on his or her ability to make very good guesses about trends and changes. The business professional's future success requires a constant environmental scan and evaluation of trends and fads. This environmental scan should reassess the application of core principles by challenging and questioning their effectiveness and relevance. Successful business practice depends upon a good work ethic and practical lifelong learning. It also doesn't hurt to have a working crystal ball.

But discussion of séance sessions aside, a business professional should always be looking to the future. What are some forms and forces for which business professionals can scan and plan?

Socio-Economic Shifts

The financial crash of 2008, like its predecessors, caused many social and economic changes in the conduct and confidence of international and national institutions and leaders. Society is understandably cautious of markets, and vice versa, as politicians seek to craft and enforce new regulations whose effects probably cannot be entirely anticipated.

On a larger scale, globalization has reshaped the roles that nations play in producing and consuming goods. In the 1950s, America was primarily a manufacturing economy with a burgeoning service sector. Now much of our manufacturing is outsourced to nations with competitive labor cost advantages, such as China and Mexico. In just fifty years, America's economic strengths changed from manufacturing and production to innovation and service.

Rapidly rising higher education costs are one area to watch. Even as politicians and parents decide that every American needs a college education, rapidly rising costs and increased student loan debt have the potential to create a bubble similar to the housing crisis of 2008 but with much more dire effects since student loan debt cannot be erased. Savvy business professionals pay attention to economic news and forecasts, and they consider the implications for their own businesses and careers.

Technological Advances

Business professionals saw a tectonic shift in the universal availability and use of technology in the first part of the twenty-first century. The changes have dramatically affected the way business professionals communicate and work in terms of efficiency and effectiveness. Information and research are available around the clock and easily obtained. Social media allows quick, casual networking.

But none of these advances has come without a cost. Just twenty-five years ago, access to information was guarded by gatekeepers who ensured that information, when you could get it, had been peer-reviewed and verified. Today, the challenge is not getting information—a Google search will give you more information on any topic from Chihuahua breeding to collateralized debt obligations than you can possibly absorb. Too much information—that's the challenge for the new millennium. How do you locate reliable information? And once you find it, what do you do with it?

Another challenge for business professionals is that they are always connected to work. I was out with friends a few weeks ago when I noticed a silence at our table, coupled with an eerie glow. Every one of us was scrolling down on our smartphones, checking work e-mails, voice mails, stock prices. Some of us were even commenting on each other's Facebook posts. Our intimate get-together was destroyed by technology.

Technology should not be your friend. It should be a tool to help you accomplish your work more efficiently. If it becomes more than that, learn to establish professional boundaries. If you are a manager, it's essential that you model those boundaries to your subordinates. You will set the tone for your organization. The business professionalism core is built on ideas of respect and balance.

Political Forces

While most Americans claim to inhabit the middle ground of political opinions, the business professional exists in a political, bipolar world in early twenty-first century. The two dominant political parties are entrenched in bitter partisan battles to stake out the most extreme opposite positions, and gridlock rules in a stagnant economy. Progressive political agendas clash with more traditional political views. The younger generations seem to support some of those progressive political aims.

But for politicians, polarization is the rule on almost any topic. Attaching blame prevails over solving problems. As a result, more and more people are simply "checking out" of so-called representative government. But a business professional cannot afford to do that. In many cases, politicians may have power to help or harm your industry. It's essential that you stay aware and informed about the issues and that you support politicians who can model professionalism instead of vitriolic mudslinging.

What political issues in this campaign cycle could potentially affect your industry? Your job? Take a few minutes to reflect on regulatory, environmental, and legal concerns that concern you personally. What can you do as a business professional to communicate your concerns to your elected officials?

Social and Demographic Shifts

Much has been written about the social and demographic shifts occurring in early twenty-first century America. Business professionals are Sociological and psychological issues are affecting entire nations as society is trying to adjust to major work and lifestyle changes at every income level.

Even as immigration becomes a hot-button issue, America is quietly becoming more racially mixed: by 2050, the Hispanic population is expected to triple. Gender roles have also changed dramatically, with more dual-income households and working mothers. In 2009, nearly half of all medical school graduates were women, up from just five percent in 1949. This increased diversity is good news for business professionals: intentional diversity is associated with an active, innovative organizational culture.

While the future may be difficult to predict, the future of diversity is not: businesses that value diversity will survive and thrive.

Risk Management and the Risk Culture

As the example of British Petroleum's 2010 oil spill demonstrates, effective risk management is an essential part of an organization's strategic plan. But how do organizations define risk? And what is risk management?

Risk is the probability of loss or harm. *Risk management* is the strategic planning and tactical decisions made to reduce, avoid, or eliminate risk and, therefore, loss or harm.

Financial risk management deals with risks inherent in financial markets and company liquidity. Operations risk management involves the actual risks of company operations. The overall ethic of risk management is referred to as the *risk culture* of a company.

Strong Risk Culture

A strong risk culture is actively engaged in risk assessment and management as part of the overall strategic plan. The general features of a strong risk culture include leadership and management. Strong leadership defines the risk culture and shares that vision with management. Leadership acts as if it believes in its vision. In the feedback cycle, leadership listens to new risks identified and responds with a course of action consistent with the culture of risk.

Management commits to the leadership's vision and manages to that standard. Teamwork is essential throughout the workforce, and management provides the regulation of the team by giving guidance, allocating resources, and monitoring deadlines.

In a strong risk culture, management trains employees to respond properly to risks, for example, wearing safety equipment or using machinery correctly. Management monitors the results of risk management tactics and accounts for poor risk-taking behaviors. Management also establishes quantitative analysis tools to measure risk culture compliance. Any problem areas are reported to leadership and discussed, and a mutually agreed upon intervention occurs.

Operational risk management concerns both management and measurement of risk. Traditionally, operations risk management involved all the company processes and systems, all employees for management and training, and any external event, such as political interference. A strong culture identifies, measures, and implements a strategy consistent with overall company goals. Of course, ongoing stewardship is required with financial risk management.

Weak Risk Culture

Weak risk cultures begin with resistant and sometimes arrogant leadership. For example, Lehman Brothers, the investment bank that filed for bankruptcy following the subprime mortgage crisis of 2008, had a weak risk culture. Management is either not informed about strategic goals or communications about those goals are not transparent.

Leadership and management must believe in and be committed to the same vision of risk culture. In a weak risk culture, new risks are not identified on a timely basis; ongoing stewardship is an essential part of a strong risk culture. Underutilizing personnel or improperly training them creates a weak risk culture operationally.

Merely considering risk avoidance and mitigation as an afterthought—a canned tagline to a strategic plan—rather than proactively seeking profitable means to deal with risk is a characteristic of a weak risk culture financially. For instance, in financial risk management, trading in derivatives can be profitable by substituting risky interest rate positions for more time-sensitive hedges.

Weak risk cultures do not think they can fail, so they don't plan. And of course, as the saying goes, failure to plan is planning to fail, especially when it comes to risk management.

Why Organizations Struggle with Risk Management

Failure to have a strong risk culture may occur for four broad reasons: board-level decisions, leadership attitudes, management failures, and unanticipated outside influences. When a strong risk culture organization struggles, communication may be to blame. Communications are an important factor in these disconnects between strong risk culture and failed operations or policies.

Arrogant leadership destroys strong risk cultures when it refuses sound advice or even ignores information. Leadership needs to listen as well as share their vision. Communication means assuring all employees are informed and understand the culture. Then, leadership must live that commitment to risk management. When the leader appears not to care, everyone will become complacent.

Unethical leadership weakens risk culture. This problem seems to occur among the greedy. Remember our sharks in the assertiveness model? Sharks misappropriate company funds or taking bonuses inappropriately; even as Lehman Brothers collapsed, top executives took large bonuses.

Since management usually controls most day-to-day activities in an organization, managers have the greatest chance of failure to manage risk. By monitoring and measuring on an ongoing basis, strong risk culture managers obtain the metrics they need to tweak policy and procedures in response to change. Failure to monitor is probably the biggest reason why risk cultures weaken over time.

Even natural disasters have an element of management. For example, management charged with locating a new plant location may fail to observe that the proposed location is in a flood plain or abuts an undesirable or incompatible neighbor. In 2010, the Fukushima nuclear power plant in Japan reached critical levels after an earthquake and tsunami damaged its coolant systems. Though Japan is one of the most technologically advanced societies in the modern world, the government was criticized for its failure to identify the potential risk to its citizens should a collapse like the one at Fukushima occur—and given the plant's location, such a collapse was probably inevitable.

In some cases, management suffers time or budget constraints and chooses shortcuts over reduced risk. Economic pressures such as new, unanticipated competitors can weaken the risk culture. For example, the competitor buys up raw materials, and management fails to respond. Management or their charges fail to follow procedures, or worse, are unprepared for an occurrence. This problem may be a result of poor training, poor management delegation, or poor anticipation.

In the case of resource management, Southwest Airlines successfully weathered a rapid and unpredicted increase in global fuel prices in 2007 by hedging its position. The fuel price increase left other carriers scrambling and even may have contributed to American Airlines parent company Pinnacle's filing for bankruptcy in 2012.

International operations experience cultural differences that require realignment of the risk culture locally. Failure to address these global issues weakens the organization's risk culture overall.

Outside influences, like political agendas, can also disturb the risk balance. Outside stakeholders do not always buy into leadership's vision, causing an imbalance. These outside influences generally are simply failures to envision new risks. One example in the higher education industry is the 2011 Gainful Employment legislation that impacts for-profit colleges and universities. Organizations that did not anticipate or plan for the proposed Department of Education rule changes found themselves scrambling when the rules, which link for-profit tuition to potential student earnings, took effect in 2011.

Summary

Risk management sounds simple in theory. The process of identifying, analyzing, reducing, avoiding, and transferring risk sounds like a good idea to everyone. But the actual business changes required to implement a strong risk culture within will demand relentless management and visionary leadership. The board of directors must allow leadership to lead and managers to manage a single-vision risk culture. Ongoing stewardship includes training, monitoring, changing procedures, and retraining employees.

Communications up and down the chain of command must be transparent and clear. Vigilant market watchers must assess the risk of new competitors, supply chain maintenance, and demand changes. Financial managers must optimize company positions to reduce risky investments and increase profits. As the entire company becomes one culture with one strong vision, they will change and grow together, better prepared to withstand the winds of future change.

The required skills to build a strong risk culture are:

- Leadership
- Management

- Communications
- Risk management; strong culture

How will you increase your level of ability in each of these skills? Consider applying the Four Pillars to the problem of risk management. The Four Pillars form a solid basis for developing a strong risk culture that is prepared for the future.

Further Reading

Ciulla, Joanne.B. "Leadership and the problem of bogus empowerment." *In Ethics: The Heart of Leadership.* Santa Barbara, CA: Greenwood Publishers, 2004.
Greenleaf, Robert K. *The Servant Leader: A Transformative Path.* Mahweh, New Jersey: Paulist Press, 1977.
Maxwell, John C. *There's No Such Thing as "Business" Ethics: There's Only One Rule for Making Decisions.* New York: AOL Time Warner, 2003.
Fink, Steven. Crisis *Management: Planning for the Inevitable.* Lincoln, NE: iUniverse, 2000.

Case Study

Your company has plans to build a new manufacturing facility and is considering three possible locations. The first location is in Fort Worth, Texas. The second location is in Ciudad Juarez, Mexico. The third location is in American Fork, Utah. Using the Internet, research each of these places and write a memo assessing the risks associated with opening a manufacturing facility in each of these places. Then make a recommendation for a site based on your initial risk assessment.

⮾ **EXERCISE** ⮾

Consider the following questions and write down your answers.

- What roles do leadership and management play in risk management?
- In your experience, which is more important to shaping an organization's risk management culture, competent managers or strategic leaders?
- What role does communication play in business professionalism as it relates to risk management?
- What role does business professionalism play in risk management? How do the Four Pillars help to craft a strong risk management culture?
- Risk management is a long-term view. How does that long-term focus conflict with project level management or modern quarterly bonus thinking? How can the conflict between these two views be reduced in magnitude?

CHAPTER 9

Creating Dialogue

Mark and Diane work in the marketing department of a shoe company that has created a new fitness athletic shoe with a special shock absorbing sole. Their supervisor tells them that they have to create a campaign that will make the new product stand out from its competition. "What if we said the shoes could help reduce cellulite?" Diane asks in a brainstorming meeting. "I bet every woman would have to have a pair." "Is it true?" Mark says. "Has the company done any studies to determine whether wearing the shoe reduces cellulite?" "Who cares?" Diane responds. "As long as they are wearing a fitness shoe, they'll probably at least think it's working." Mark has concerns about Diane's plan. Though it tests well with focus groups, he just doesn't feel right.

Business professionalism builds from the ground up. It depends on a dialogue between stakeholders.

Now that you've learned the Four Pillars, how can you share them with your colleagues? This chapter will give you some talking points to start the conversation that could change your organization.

Theory (Ideals)

When we talk about business professionalism, we're really talking about the modern manifestation of a very old idea: ethics. Ethics are an inquiry into moral judgments, standards, and rules of conduct. The foundation of business professionalism is core values. Standards and rules of conduct imply codification of morals, and societies do build moral standards into law. The Ten Commandments are an example of codified moral standards. Most modern organizations, especially publicly traded companies, have crafted a business code of ethics that their employees are expected to follow.

Talking Point: Ethics in Marketing

How do you market a product or service ethically? What is the balance between full-disclosure honesty and keeping trade secrets? What are ethical communications? Apply this marketing discussion to all communications: internal, external, and personal.

A review of ethics requires a review of certain principles and rules. The following list is from Gene Laczniak's, "Frameworks for Analyzing Marketing Ethics":

The Golden Rule states ethical behavior treatment is based on how the actor would want to be treated.

- The utilitarian principle implies ethical behavior is a result of the greatest good for the greatest number of people, and by extension, the least amount of bad.
- Kant's categorical imperative demands to act so that the action, under the circumstances, could be a universal ethical law or standard of behavior.
- The professional ethic requires action that would be viewed as proper by a peer review process.
- The TV test relies on management reflecting on a TV interview and asking, "Would I be comfortable explaining to a national TV audience why I took this action?"

Modern business may well be wedded to the mass media test. Mass media is visually driven and relentless. Business professionalism demands knowledge and skill in handling social media. The TV test relies on management reflecting on a TV interview and asking, "Would I be comfortable explaining to a national TV audience why I took this action?" The modern world of video and the immediate news cycle creates a new "ethic" for organizations. This ethic implies that the consequences of actions are less important than the explanation for public consumption. The new ethicist is the "spin doctor."

The utilitarian principle implies that the end is more important than the means in ethical behavior, a more situational ethic. Many business professionals use some form of utilitarian ethics in their day-to-day decision making.

The other rules or theories consider behavior to be moral or immoral and results to be less controllable by the actor.

Behavior-based ethics are referred to as deontological (Kant), while the results or consequence theories are teleological (Bentham and Mills).

Teleological Ethics

The teleological, or consequence-driven, ethics involve the utilitarian principle. Essentially, this focus on the greatest good for the greatest number insinuates that the ends justify the means, implying that someone determines what is best for the most people and what hurt tolerance is acceptable for the remainder. The individual perspective drives these utility decisions more so than a central decision maker can determine.

The utilitarian principle implies ethical behavior is a result of the greatest good for the greatest number of people; therefore, if one group considers the consequences bad, that group should take heart in the assumption that all other groups did better. Good was maximized at the expense of the one group. The relative importance to each group must be assessed to make a rational decision.

The consequences-based ethic framework—teleological— concerns four data points:

1. Perceived consequences for considered actions
2. Probability that consequences will affect the stakeholder group
3. The good or bad of each consequence
4. The relative importance of each group

As you can see, these data are exceedingly subjective. The perceived consequences of any action are likely to be an incomplete list at best and in polar opposition to reality at worst. Intent and reality can differ; intent is deontological in nature. Actions, no matter what their intent, do in fact lead to consequences.

Deontological Ethics

While teleological ethics looks at ends and greatest goods, Kant's categorical imperative demands us to act so that any action, under the circumstances, could be a universal ethical law or standard of behavior. This moral absolutism suggests that the ethic is the only relevant concern. Consequence is an unimportant result of morality.

As an example, if you lit a fire in your neighbor's fireplace because you wanted him to come home to a warm house (a good ethical intent), but a spark escaped and burned the house down (a bad outcome), you would still have acted ethically. Your intent was good, irrespective of a bad outcome.

Business professional ethics require action that would be viewed as proper by a peer review. This is arrogance, at the very least. The ethics of the peers take precedence over the ethic of other people or the consequence bestowed upon them. The group ethic of professionals is more learned or appropriate than the masses. The consequences of this professional action are not mentioned in this ethical model.

Summary

As we noted earlier, organizational ethics is utilitarian, serving many concerns: economic implications, organizational expectations, and effects on stakeholders are all considered in choosing a course of action.

From the decision makers' point of view, the considerations are: individual ethics, organizational expectations, and professional ethics. Within an organizational structure, ethical questions are individually decided and then reviewed within the professional and organizational code of ethics to decide which alternative is the best choice.

The Four Pillars serve as a framework within a utilitarian model. They can be adapted to situations and stakeholders.

Case Study

For this book, we defined *business professionalism* as a business-like mindset or judgment system based on self-developed and managed knowledge, skills, attitudes, and behaviors that is influenced by work ethic, talent/ability, experience, and the environment. That working definition guided and informed the rest of the book. It was a working definition because readers of this book will use it as a yardstick in terms of creating their own working definition based on their worldview and experiences.

Now that you have read the book and learned the Four Pillars of business professionalism, read and respond to this question:

We have all looked at the appearances and behaviors of business people and thought, "I wish that person were more professional." What does that mean? Is it conduct? Is it appearance? Is it bearing? Is it rational thinking and behavior? Stoicism/self-discipline? Appropriateness? Standards? Trust? What?

Further Reading

Bennis, Warren G., Parikh, Jagdish, and Lessem, Ronnie, *Beyond Leadership: Balancing Economics, Ethics and Ecology,* Blackwell Publishers, 1994.

Clegg, Stewart, Kornberger, Martin, and Rhodes, Carl. "Business Ethics as Practice." *British Journal of Management, 18,* 2007, 107–122.

Karnes, R. "A Change in Business Ethics: The Impact on Employer–Employee Relations. *Journal of Business Ethics,* 87, no. 2, 2009, 189-197.

Senge, Peter M. *The Fifth Discipline: The Art and Practice of the Learning Organization.* New York: Doubleday, 1990.

Trevino, Linda K. and Nelson, Katherine A. *Managing Business Ethics: Straight Talk About How To Do It Right.* 4th ed. Hoboken, NJ: John Wiley & Sons, Inc., 2007.

Laczniak, Gene. "Frameworks for Analyzing Marketing Ethics." *Journal of Macromarketing,*3, no.1, 1983, 7-13.

⸎ EXERCISE ⸎

Take a few hours to develop a personal professional development roadmap with goals and timelines utilizing Appendix F.

Share your responses with some people you trust in order to start a discussion.

CHAPTER 10

Building a Code
of Ethics

Karen left a Fortune 500 company to start a small business that connects service providers with customers through an online referral service. She has just hired her first five employees, all of whom are friends or former business associates. In their first staff meeting, she brings up the subject of creating a code of ethics that will outline expectations and provide consequences for unethical behavior. "We all trust each other," her office manager says. "Why do we need a formal code? We don't want to be like a big, faceless corporation."

We all know that publicly traded companies must have well-established codes of business ethics and practices. But does a small organization like Karen's need a code of ethics? The answer is a resounding yes. And as Karen realized, the first step to creating an effective code of ethics is involving the stakeholders. The final chapter of this book is concerned with building a code of ethics that incorporates the Four Pillars of business professionalism.

Taylor, in his *Principles of Ethics: An Introduction to Ethics* (1975), defines ethics as an "inquiry into the nature and grounds of morality where morality is taken to mean moral judgments, standards and rules of conduct." Ethics codify morals with "standards and rules of conduct." Societies, whether through governments, guilds, or professional boards, do reflect moral standards in law.

Major corporations, smaller companies, civic organizations, and professional organizations all have codes of ethics. Definitive by nature, codes of ethics explain the beliefs inherent in your profession and what behavior your stakeholders can expect from you.

Implied by membership in the profession are expectations regarding your individual business professional behavior, your beliefs, and who you are.

Generally, a code of ethics derives from an agreement among stakeholders in the business: owners, bosses, employees, customers, suppliers, and the legal and regulatory environment. The following are some suggestions for creating a code of ethics that reflects your vision and intentional worldview.

Individualize Your Code

Since your code of ethics reflects a moral agreement among your stakeholders, it should be unique. What makes your code of ethics specific to your organization other than the title or the logo? Within an industry certain similarities will exist, but focus on those ethics that differentiate your business from the competition. For example, Apple holds its production facilities in China to a higher standard of workplace safety than is required by local laws. That focus has paid off in the company's public relations.

Involve Stakeholders

Do you want a high level of acceptance and adherence to your code? Do you want to avoid nitpicking revisions of wording after the code is published? Then get stakeholder buy-in from the start. Karen realized the importance of establishing a code of ethics at the very start. As the leader of her organization, she also has the responsibility to help stakeholders understand the importance of an established code. The more actively involved the stakeholders are in forming this agreement, the more easily the code is to enforce. Employees view company behavior differently than suppliers, but both views are valuable, and usually foreign, to managers. Key obligations from the stakeholders' perspective will be revealed. Also, remember to periodically assess your code for weakness. Again, this assessment should involve shareholder input.

Find Good Examples

You don't want to copy someone else's code—that would be unethical—but learning the scope and depth of a well-written code of ethics by examining what other organizations have done will assist you in the process. Individualize your code, and stick to a clear, concise, readable style.

The basics of any code of ethics include the following:

1. Define ethical standards and to whom this behavior is owed.

2. Define conflicts of interest and how they are to be avoided.
3. Define the duty to safeguard company assets.
4. Define the duty to protect proprietary information. What constitutes improper use and access?
5. Define the duty to protect confidential records.
6. Define respect for and intentional pursuit of diversity in your workplace.

You might also want to consider the political implications of company employee activity to avoid the appearance of conflicts of interest. Some company leaders are iconic. When Donald Trump enters the Republican presidential primary, it is assumed that the entire Trump organization is Republican. A good code of ethics clearly defines and regulates this separation between company business and outside activities.

Scope

Your code explains governance with clarity. Be specific.

- Who is expected to honor the code?
- Are there specific sections for different levels of employees, or does everyone follow one code?
- Who signs the agreement? Whether metaphoric or in reality, who is agreeing to this code?

Implementation

How will these values translate into practical action? A well-crafted code speaks to employee and supervisory behavior. What can everyone expect?

- Education: will new employees receive training regarding the code's requirements? Will current employees? Will there be ongoing refresher courses?
- Enforcement: is the code a guiding document or strictly enforceable? If it is strictly enforceable, be very specific. Who intervenes or enforces it? Is there supervisory enforcement or a panel of stakeholders?

Set a Termination Date

Aren't ethics "carved in stone"? The answer is, not really. Times change, conditions change, and refreshing the discussion must be scheduled or it may be ignored, until a crisis precipitates a review. Crisis situations are not the time to completely overhaul the code of ethics. Periodic review—the self-management pillar—will ensure that your code of ethics stays complete, concise, and relevant.

Summary

A code of ethics is a powerful document for defining your organization's position regarding business professionalism. Crafting and implementing a code that is based on the Four Pillars of professional formation, self-management, presence/image, and communication will demonstrate your organization's commitment to acting with integrity.

But the code cannot be a merely a collection of words—it must be a call to action that is lived and practiced daily by every business professional in your organization. No matter where your career is today, you can help your organization improve by taking an active role in modeling and assessing your code of ethics.

If your organization does not yet have a formal code, encourage management to develop and implement one. Meanwhile, continue to practice the Four Pillars in your own personal code of ethics.

Business professionalism has the potential to change the world of work. As organizations commit to ethical, professional behavior, they will see increased productivity, efficiency, and morale in their workplaces. And ethical organizations start with ethical individuals like you.

You've finished the book. Now go out and live it.

Further Reading

Gilley, K. Matthew, Robertson, Christopher J., and Mazur, Tim C. "The Bottom-Line Benefits of Ethics Code Commitment." *Business Horizons* 53, no. 1, 2010, 31-37.

Messikomer, Carla, and Cirka, Carol. "Constructing a Code of Ethics: An Experiential Case of a National Professional Organization." *Journal of Business Ethics* 95, no. 1, 2010, 55-71.

Spiro, Josh. *"How to Write a Code of Ethics for Business."* Inc. Magazine Online, 2010.

Taylor, Paul. *Principles of Ethics: An Introduction to Ethics*, Dickinson, 1975.

Spiro, Josh. *"How to Write a Code of Ethics for Business."* Inc. Magazine Online (2010).

⤎ EXERCISE ⤏

Consider the discussion of ethics in Chapter 9. What ethical standard makes the most long-term sense for businesses? Where do your personal ethics fit into these theories? Are ethics universal? Write a personal code of ethics that reflects your beliefs.

Bibliography

Aristotle. *Nichomachean Ethics.*

Aristotle. *The Art of Rhetoric.*

Arum, Richard and Roksa, Josipa. *Academically Adrift: Limited Learning on College Campus.* Chicago: University of Chicago Press, 2010.

Bennis, Warren G. *On Becoming a Leader* (4th ed.). Philadelphia: Basic Books, 2010.

Bennis, Warren G., Parikh, Jagdish, and Lessem, Ronnie, *Beyond Leadership: Balancing Economics, Ethics and Ecology,* Blackwell Publishers, 1994.

Cardon, Peter W. and Okoro, Ephraim A. "Focus on Business Practices: Professional Characteristics Communicated by Formal Versus Casual Workplace Attire." *Business Communication Quarterly* 72, 2009, 355.

Ciulla, Joanne B. "Leadership and the problem of bogus empowerment." *In Ethics: The Heart of Leadership.* Santa Barbara, CA: Greenwood Publishers, 2004.

Clegg, Stewart, Kornberger, Martin, and Rhodes, Carl. "Business Ethics as Practice." *British Journal of Management* 18, 2007, 107–122.

Collins, James. *Good to Great: Why Some Companies Make the Leap... And Others Don't.* New York: Harper Collins, 2001.

Covey, Stephen R., *The 7 Habits of Highly Effective People: Restoring the Character Ethic,* New York: Simon & Schuster, 1990.

Daft, Richard L. *The Leadership Experience* (4th ed.). Mason, OH: Thomson/Cengage, 2008.

Dembinski, Paul H., Lager, Carol., Cornford, Andrew, and Bonvin, Jean-Michel (eds.). *Enron and World Finance: A Case Study in Ethics*. New York: Palgrave, 2006.

Fink, Steven. *Crisis Management: Planning for the Inevitable*. Lincoln, NE: iUniverse, 2000.

Gerson, Sharon J. Gerson, Steven M. *Workplace Communication: Process and Product*. Upper Saddle River, NJ: Pearson Prentice Hall, 2007.

Gigerenzer, Gerd and Selten, Reinhard. *Bounded Rationality*. Cambridge: MIT Press, 2002.

Gilbert, Daniel. *Stumbling on Happiness*, New York: Knopf, 2006.

Gilley, K. Matthew, Robertson, Christopher J., and Mazur, Tim C. "The Bottom-Line Benefits of Ethics Code Commitment." *Business Horizons* 53, no. 1, 2010, 31-37.

Gladwell, Malcolm. *Blink: The Power of Thinking without Thinking*. New York: Little,

Brown and Company, 2005.

Goleman, Daniel, *Emotional Intelligence*, New York: Bantam, 1997.

Greenleaf, Robert K. *The Servant Leader: A Transformative Path*. Mahweh, New Jersey:

Paulist Press, 1977.

Gunn, Tim and Moloney, Kate. *Tim Gunn: A Guide to Quality, Taste, and Style*. New York: Abrams Image, 2007.

Heath, Chip and Heath, Dan. *Made to Stick: Why Some Ideas Survive and Others Die*. New York: Random House, 2007.

Huevel, Katrina. *Meltdown: How Greed and Corruption Shattered our Financial System and*

How We Can Recover. New York: Nation Books, 2009.

Kahneman, Daniel. "Maps of Bounded Rationality: Psychology for Behavioral Economics." *The American Economic Review*, 93, no. 5, 2003, 1449-75.

Kahneman, Daniel., Diener, Ed., & Schwarz, Norbert (eds). *Well-Being: The Foundations of Hedonic Psychology.* New York: Russell Sage Foundation, 2003.

Karnes, R. "A Change in Business Ethics: The Impact on Employer–Employee Relations. *Journal of Business Ethics,* 87, no. 2, 2009, 189-197.

Kouzes, James and Posner, Barry. *The Leadership Challenge.* San Francisco: Jossey-Bass, 2008

Laczniak, Gene. "Frameworks for Analyzing Marketing Ethics." *Journal of Macromarketing,*3, no.1, 1983, 7-13.

Maxwell, John C. *There's No Such Thing as "Business" Ethics: There's Only One Rule forMaking Decisions.* New York: AOL Time Warner, 2003.

Messikomer, Carla, and Cirka, Carol. "Constructing a Code of Ethics: An Experiential Case of a National Professional Organization." *Journal of Business Ethics* 95, no. 1, 2010, 55-71.

Osborne, Martin J. *An Introduction to Game Theory,* Oxford: Oxford University Press, 2004.

Peluchette, Joy V. and Karl, Katherine. "The impact of work-place attire on employee self-perceptions." *Human Resource Development Quarterly* 18, no.3, 2007, 345-360.

Project Management Institute. *A Guide to the Project Management Body of Knowledge*
(3rd ed. ed.). Project Management Institute, 2003.

Rousseau, Jean-Jacques, *'The Social Contract' and Other Later Political Writings,* trans.

Victor Gourevitch. Cambridge: Cambridge University Press, 1997.

Schein, Edgar H., *The Corporate Culture Survival Guide,* A Warren Bennis Book, San Francisco: Jossey-Bass, Inc., 1999.

Schwartz, Barry. *The Paradox of Choice,* New York: Harper Perennial, 2004.

Senge, Peter M. *The Fifth Discipline: The Art and Practice of the Learning Organization.*
New York: Doubleday, 1990.

Simon, Herbert. "A Behavioral Model of Rational Choice," in *Models of Man, Social and Rational: Mathematical Essays on Rational Human Behavior in a Social Setting.* New York: Wiley, 1957.

Smith, Adam. *An Inquiry into the Nature and Causes of the Wealth of Nations.* Chicago, IL: University of Chicago Press, 1952.

Solow, Robert M. *The New Industrial State or Son of Affluence.* Indianapolis: Bobbs-Merrill, 1967.

Spiro, Josh. "How to Write a Code of Ethics for Business." Inc. Magazine Online, 2010.

Swedberg, Richard. "The Structure of Confidence and the Collapse of Lehman Brothers," in M. Lounsbury, P. M. Hirsch (ed.) *Markets on Trial: The Economic Sociology of the U.S. Financial Crisis: Part A (Research in the Sociology of Organizations, Volume 30),* Emerald Group, Publishing Limited, 2010, 71-114.

Taylor, Paul. *Principles of Ethics: An Introduction to Ethics, Dickinson, 1975.*

Toulmin, Stephen. *The Uses of Argument.* Cambridge: Cambridge University Press, 1958.

Trevino, Linda K. and Nelson, Katherine A. *Managing Business Ethics: Straight Talk About How To Do It Right.* 4th ed. Hoboken, NJ: John Wiley & Sons, Inc., 2007.

Appendix A—Pillar One (Professional Formation) Action Plan

Existing	Gap	Desired	Action Plan

Notes

Appendix B—Pillar Two (Professional Self-Management) Action Plan

Existing	Gap	Desired	Action Plan

Notes

Appendix C—Pillar Three (Professional Presence/Image) Action Plan

Existing	Gap	Desired	Action Plan

Notes

Appendix D—Pillar Four (Professional Communication) Action Plan

Existing	Gap	Desired	Action Plan

Notes

Appendix E—Assertiveness Evaluation

Existing	Gap	Desired	Action Plan
Self			
Close Relationships			
Groups			
Society			

Notes

Appendix F—Professional Development Roadmap

Existing	Gap	Desired	Action Plan

Notes

Appendix G—Individual Reflection Assessment

Existing	Gap	Desired	Action Plan

Notes

Appendix H—Master/Peer Assessment Action Plan

Existing	Gap	Desired	Action Plan

Notes

Appendix I—360-Degree Assessment Action Plan

Existing	Gap	Desired	Action Plan

Notes

Appendix J—Worldview Development Action Plan

Existing	Gap	Desired	Action Plan

Notes

Appendix K—Personal Core Development Action Plan

Existing	Gap	Desired	Action Plan

Notes

CPSIA information can be obtained
at www.ICGtesting.com
Printed in the USA
LVHW01s2220251217
560740LV00012B/217/P

9 781475 017281